BARRON'S Let's Prepare for the

PARCC

GRADE 6 ELA/LITERACY TEST

MaryBeth Estok, M.Ed.

About the Author

MaryBeth Estok taught sixth-grade language arts for eight years at George Washington Middle School in Wayne, New Jersey. She served on several curriculum committees that integrated the district's writing and reading programs and aligned the programs with the New Jersey Core Curriculum Content Standards. Ms. Estok has also written other test prep books: Barron's *New Jersey NJASK 6* and *New Jersey Grade 6 ELA/Literacy Tests*. Before teaching middle school, Ms. Estok taught language arts, math, science, and social studies to fifth graders for seven years.

Acknowledgments

I would like to thank my family, friends, and especially my husband, Joe, for supporting me in this venture. I would also like to thank Peter Mavrikis for his support and guidance.

All inquiries should be addressed to:
Barron's Educational Series, Inc.
250 Wireless Boulevard
Hauppauge, NY 11788
www.barronseduc.com

ISBN: 978-1-4380-0817-2

Library of Congress Control Number: 2016936464

Date of Manufacture: June 2016
Manufactured by: B11R11

Printed in the United States of America

9 8 7 6 5 4 3 2 1

10% POST-CONSUMER WASTE
Paper contains a minimum of 10% post-consumer waste (PCW). Paper used in this book was derived from certified, sustainable forestlands.

Contents

Note to Students

What do you look forward to during your sixth-grade year? Dances? Maybe. Field trips? Usually. Spending time with friends? Definitely. Taking the English Language Arts/Literacy Test? Probably not. Why is this the case? Well, after preparing for months, you are expected to concentrate for hours at a time on different topics and remember everything you have learned over the course of the year. The fact is that this test is a way to show what you know. Teachers and parents tell you that the test is important, you should give your best effort, and keep going even when you feel your brain cannot possibly think any more. *WOW!* This is easier said than done, right? Is there a magic potion that you can take and then—*poof*—the stress goes away? Sadly, there isn't. But we can help!

This book has been written for you, the sixth-grade student. It cannot promise to make all of the stress magically go away, but the tips and practice exercises can help to increase your confidence. Confidence is one of the keys to performing better on the Grade 6 English Language Arts/Literacy Test. The book explains everything you will need to know about the test.

You might be wondering why you even have to take this test in the first place. You also may be wondering what kinds of questions will be on the test. Well, this book gives you the answers to these two questions and more. By the time you are done working with it, you will have learned about the three major parts of the PARCC (Partnership for Assessment of Readiness for College and Careers) Assessment: the Narrative Writing Task, the Literary Analysis Task, and the Research Simulation Task. The chapters describe each section of the test. Examples are also provided so you can practice what you have learned. The last chapter provides two sample timed tests for the best practice possible. The answers are provided so you can check to see how well you have done. So let's get started!

> **IMPORTANT NOTE:** Barron's has made every effort to ensure the content of this book is accurate as of press time, but the PARCC Assessments are constantly changing. Be sure to consult *www.parcconline.org* for all the latest testing information. Regardless of the changes that may be announced after press time, this book will still provide a strong framework for sixth-grade students preparing for the assessment.

PARCC Test Overview

It's springtime, the weather is beginning to get nicer, students get to enjoy recess outside again, and everyone seems to be in a better mood. That mood quickly changes when the teacher makes the statement that no student wants to hear: "The PARCC assessment is coming up soon." Immediately after the groans from children everywhere, the panic begins to set in. Why in the world does the state make students take this test? In this chapter you will get the answer to that question and probably many others that you may have about the test.

In this chapter you will:

- read a description of the Grade 6 PARCC English Language Arts/Literacy Test;
- find out about the parts of the test;
- learn how the test is scored;
- discover how to prepare yourself for the test;
- review types of computer-based questions; and
- review working with multiple-choice questions.

Please be advised that the actual assessments are computer-based, so we have adapted some of the sample questions to work in this book format. To show this in some circumstances, you will see the computer-based question followed by a similar question in parentheses that instructs you to write an answer in this book. For example:

Highlight all of the details that support your answer to Part A. (In this case, write the details that support your answer to Part A on the lines provided.)

Understanding the Grade 6 PARCC
English Language Arts/Literacy Test

What is the PARCC anyway? Well, your state is now part of the Partnership for Assessment of Readiness for College and Careers (PARCC). This group is made up of educators from several states who work together to make sure that students leaving high school are ready to be successful in college and their careers. In order to do this, the group has developed an assessment to see if students at each grade level have mastered certain skills that are listed in the Common Core State Standards. These standards are skills and concepts that the state believes you should possess and understand at the end of each grade. Basically, it's everything you should know by the end of the school year.

Students at each grade level must take a standardized test. Standardized tests are taken by many students at the same time and scored according to a set of standards, or rules. This year you will be taking the PARCC assessment for language arts. This assessment will take place after you have completed about 75 percent to 90 percent of the school year.

Can this book give you the exact questions on the tests so you can memorize the answers? Sorry, but the answer is no. No one is allowed to see the test before the testing date. Not even your parents or teachers. What we do know is the *types* of questions that are on the test. We can use similar questions to help prepare you for the tests.

Organization of the Assessment

The assessment will be computer-based. This means that you will take the test on the computer. This may be a totally new experience for you. When you log in to the test, you will read directions that will guide you through what you need to know about using the computer to complete the test. After that, you will be instructed to begin the test. Always follow your teacher's instructions for how to complete the PARCC Assessment. He or she will guide you through the entire process.

The assessment has three units. For each part, you will read at least one passage and then respond to questions. These questions may be in different forms. For example, questions may take the form of multiple-choice, drag and drop, or select from a list. Each section also has a question that will require you to respond in essay form. The total time of the test will be 5 hours and 10 minutes for all three units. You will have 110 minutes to complete Unit 1. You will also have 110 minutes to complete Unit 2. The first section of the assessment is the **Literary Analysis Task**. Here you will read excerpts from more than one book or poem. You will answer questions based on the individual passages and analyze the texts and respond in essay form. You will have 90 minutes to complete Unit 3.

The second section is the **Research Simulation Task**. In this section, you will be viewing three sources of nonfiction information. This information is presented in different forms, such as articles, political cartoons, pictures, or videos. After viewing the information, you will be asked to write an analytical essay in which you make a claim and support your opinion by including information from the sources.

The final section of the test is the **Narrative Writing Task**. After reading a passage, you will answer questions and then write a narrative based on the text.

PARCC Changes

The 2015 ELA PARCC involved two parts. The first part was the Performance-Based Assessment (PBA), which was given after about 75 percent of the school year was completed. The students then took the End-of-Year (EOY) assessment after about 90 percent of the school year was completed. Soon after the testing was done, the PARCC committee decided to change the format of the 2016 PARCC test. The length of the Language Arts Assessment was decreased by 30 minutes. Also, both the PBA and EOY tests were combined into one, which will be given sometime after 75 percent of the school year has been completed. The PARCC assessment is continually being evaluated and therefore the format may have been modified since this book has been printed. Please check *www.parcconline.org* for the most up-to-date information about the PARCC.

Working with Computer-Based Questions

There are three types of questions that you will probably see on the test that may be new to you. Each question will be on the right side of the computer screen. The passage will be on the left. You can refer back to the passage at any time by using the scroll bar.

The first type of question is an Evidence-Based Constructed Response (EBCR). This type of question has two parts. Part A is a multiple-choice question based on the passage. For Part B, you must provide evidence to support your answer for Part A. Here's an example:

Today, you will read and think about the passage from the novel titled *Boy's Life* and the fable "Emancipation: A Life Fable." As you read these texts, you will gather information and answer questions about comparing themes and topics so you can write an essay.

Read the passage from the novel titled *Boy's Life*. Then answer the questions.

from *Boy's Life*
by Robert McCammon

1. TICK . . . TICK . . . TICK.

2. In spite of what the calendar says, I have always counted the last day of school as the first day of summer. The sun had grown steadily hotter and hung longer in the sky, the earth had greened and the sky had cleared of all but the fleeciest of clouds, the heat panted for attention like a dog who knows his day is coming, the baseball field had been mowed and white-lined and the swimming pool newly painted and filled, and as our homeroom teacher, Mrs. Selma Neville, intoned about what a good year this had been and how much we'd learned, we students who had passed through the ordeal of final exams sat with one eye fixed to the clock.

3. *Tick . . . tick . . . tick.*

4. Have mercy.

Part A

Read the sentence from paragraph 5 in the passage from *Boy's Life*.

> The world was out there, waiting beyond the square metal-rimmed windows.

How does the sentence help develop the plot of the excerpt?

○ A. It presents the climax.

○ B. It represents the conflict.

○ C. It indicates how the action changes.

○ D. It establishes how the speaker learns a lesson.

Part B

Which detail from the passage best supports the answer to Part A?

○ A. "The sun had grown steadily hotter . . . ."

○ B. ". . . the baseball field had been mowed . . . ."

○ C. ". . . and how much we'd learned . . ."

○ D. ". . . sat with one eye fixed to the clock."

The second type of question that you may see is a Technology-Enhanced Constructed Response Question (TECR). The TECR will either ask you to click, highlight, select, and/or drag and drop responses. In the following TECR example, students are asked to drag and drop details into the correct spaces.

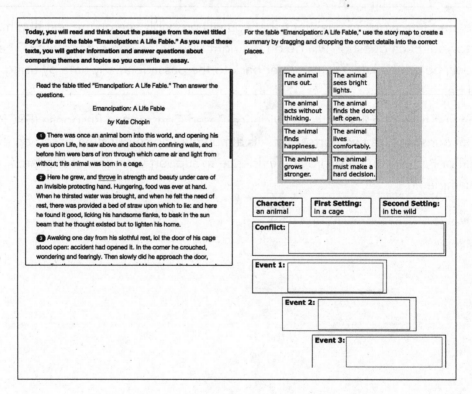

Today, you will read and think about the passage from the novel titled *Boy's Life* and the fable "Emancipation: A Life Fable." As you read these texts, you will gather information and answer questions about comparing themes and topics so you can write an essay.

Read the fable titled "Emancipation: A Life Fable." Then answer the questions.

Emancipation: A Life Fable
by Kate Chopin

1. There was once an animal born into this world, and opening his eyes upon Life, he saw above and about him confining walls, and before him were bars of iron through which came air and light from without; this animal was born in a cage.

2. Here he grew, and throve in strength and beauty under care of an invisible protecting hand. Hungering, food was ever at hand. When he thirsted water was brought, and when he felt the need of rest, there was provided a bed of straw upon which to lie: and here he found it good, licking his handsome flanks, to bask in the sun beam that he thought existed but to lighten his home.

3. Awaking one day from his slothful rest, lo! the door of his cage stood open: accident had opened it. In the corner he crouched, wondering and fearingly. Then slowly did he approach the door,

For the fable "Emancipation: A Life Fable," use the story map to create a summary by dragging and dropping the correct details into the correct places.

The animal runs out.	The animal sees bright lights.
The animal acts without thinking.	The animal finds the door left open.
The animal finds happiness.	The animal lives comfortably.
The animal grows stronger.	The animal must make a hard decision.

Character: an animal **First Setting:** in a cage **Second Setting:** in the wild

Conflict:

Event 1:

Event 2:

Event 3:

A third type of question is a Prose Constructed Response (PCR). You will see this type of question as part of the Narrative Task, the Literary Analysis Task, and Research Simulation Task. The following example is a Literary Analysis question.

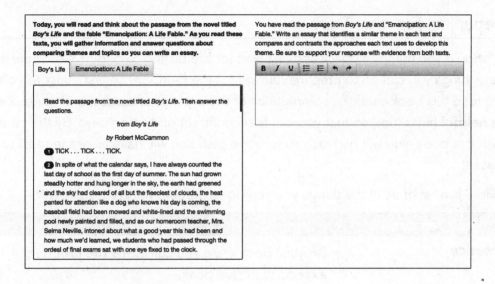

How the Test Is Scored

You may be wondering, "What happens if I fail the test? Will I have to repeat sixth grade?" The good news is you really can't fail this test. It is not the kind of test where you can get a grade of 100 percent or 25 percent. In fact, you probably won't get every single question perfectly correct. Your job is to do the best you can and earn as many points as you can. You can do this by answering the questions to the best of your ability. Each correct question earns you points.

You should try really hard to concentrate while taking the PARCC Assessment. This can be really difficult, especially if you get nervous or you begin to get tired. Remember to keep going because the results will be worth it. Most students will do this. However, there are some students who either guess on everything, don't care about their answers, or think about what they will be doing on the weekend instead of concentrating on the test and their answers. There are other students who give up and then just type anything when they get too tired or nervous. These types of students may get a lower score than they would have if they tried harder. The important thing to remember is to try your best so that the results are accurate, or really show what you know. Your teachers and principal will look at the results of the PARCC and assume that this is how much you have learned during sixth grade. You can do it, but you have to prepare!

Preparing for the Test

So, should you merely sit back and just wait for the testing to begin? No! There are many things you can do to prepare yourself for the PARCC. The first thing you can do is to read this book carefully, complete all of the practice exercises, and remember the **helpful hints** (tips) so that you can feel confident on testing days. By the time you finish this book, you will be ready to take the test. You will have all of the tools to do well!

Here is a list of all of the things you can do to prepare for the test:

What You Can Do	How?
Practice	• Do your best when you complete the practice exercises in this book.
	• Review the answers carefully. If you answered correctly, congratulate yourself! If not, read the explanations carefully and go back to see where you went wrong. Don't get discouraged. Learn from your mistakes!
Be Mentally Prepared	• Get a good night's sleep the night before testing so that you are wide awake and ready to concentrate.
	• Eat a good breakfast on the morning of a testing day to make sure you have energy. You will also be able to concentrate more on the test if you don't have to concentrate on your stomach growling.
Remember and Relax	• Listen to your teacher's advice and remember what you have learned. Your teacher has given you the tools to do well.
	• Take a deep breath if you get very nervous. Some nerves may be good, but being too nervous can stop you from concentrating on the test. Remind yourself that you are prepared for this test. You have completed this book and are ready to do a great job!

Working with Multiple-Choice Questions

The PARCC test contains multiple-choice questions. This type of question can confuse some students. There are some things you can do to perform better on these types of questions. First, make sure you read the question carefully. Sometimes you miss important parts of the question if you read it too quickly. Words like *best* or *not* can change the meaning of or the answer to a question. For example, read this question: *Which of the following is **not** a setting of the story?* Some students who don't read carefully might not see the word **not** in the sentence and will look for an example of the setting, which would lead to a wrong answer. Read the question and then ask yourself if you really understand it. If not, read it again. Once you do know what it is asking, then you can fill in the answer.

Sometimes you might understand what the question is asking, but you are not sure of the correct answer. Usually it is best to go with your first instinct, or gut feeling. If you read the question too many times, or second guess yourself, you are liable to choose the wrong answer. You may be saying, "But what if I don't even have a gut feeling? Should I just take any guess?" The answer is no. You shouldn't just try an *eeny-meeny-miney-moe* approach. This usually won't help. What you can do is try to eliminate as many of the possible answers as you can and then make an educated guess from the remaining answers. You can sometimes eliminate one or two answers that can't possibly be the answer for one reason or another. Then at least you can make an educated guess from the other two choices either by going back to the passage or by using your common sense. Here is an example:

What is a conjunction?

- ○ A. a chicken
- ○ B. your name
- ○ C. a word that connects two ideas
- ○ D. a pencil

Even if you don't know what a conjunction is, you should be able to eliminate answer (B). You probably know that it isn't a pencil or chicken either. Therefore, the correct answer must be (C). All questions might not be this easy, but you can use the strategy to help you find an answer. Just remember, if you have to go through this process, don't take too long. The PARCC is a timed test. If you are taking too long, you can skip the question and come back to it later if you have time.

Here are a few tips for answering multiple-choice questions:

- Read the question carefully and look for important words like *not* or *best*, which could change the meaning of the question. Make sure you understand the meaning of the question.
- If you don't know the answer, try to eliminate answers that don't make sense or that you know cannot be the answer.
- Remember that you will be taking a timed test, so try not to spend too much time on one test question.
- Make sure that you understand what's required in your answer. Sometimes the question may ask you to give the **two** best choices, and not just one.

CHAPTER 2

Reading for Meaning

The PARCC assessment is a computer-based test with a lot of reading. It is important that you are able to read and understand all of the texts provided.

In this chapter you will

- learn how to gain the most from a passage;
- review some sample passages; and
- read about PARCC multiple-choice questions.

How to Gain the Most from a Passage

You will find a variety of types of passages on the PARCC. They will most likely be authentic texts, in other words, passages from real books or real stories that you can find in a bookstore or online. These texts can be fiction or nonfiction. For fiction, you may be asked to read a selection from a novel, a poem, or a short story. For nonfiction, you may be asked to read a section of a biography, an article, or even a blog. A blog is a Web page that is continually updated by a person or group on a particular topic. It is often written informally. No matter what type of text you are asked to read, it is important that you understand what the author is trying to say.

There are a few ways to help yourself comprehend and remember the content of the text. On past paper-and-pencil assessments, you may have read the passage questions first and then read the passage in its entirety. You can still do that on this test.

In addition, on past assessments you may have underlined words or phrases in the passage that you thought were important. You can't exactly do that on the PARCC, but you can highlight words and take notes on the passages. To highlight words in the passage, use your mouse. As you do this, you will see three icons pop up. There are two colors for highlighting different parts of the text. For example, you may want to highlight important words in one color and plot elements in another. Simply click on a box to choose the color. The third icon is used to remove any part of the highlight that you no longer want.

There is also a notepad icon at the top of the screen. You can click on it to add notes. Each page on the assessment has a new notes page. Your notes can help you to remember important parts of the story or article.

Overall, it is very important to read carefully and do your best to focus on the passage. Read all directions and introductions carefully. Try to keep in mind the type of text you are viewing. Is it a blog? Is it nonfiction? A chart or graph? When you keep the type of text in mind, it helps you to think about your purpose for reading and what to expect from that type of text. You can review the text as many times as you wish, but keep in mind that the PARCC is a timed test. You don't want to spend too much time reviewing a passage.

Sample Passages and Questions

Since reading comprehension is such an important part of the PARCC, it is best to begin reviewing your reading skills immediately. Now you will have the opportunity to read four passages and answer questions about them. The correct answers and explanations can be found at the end of this section. Check your answers to see how well you did. If you answered correctly, congratulate yourself. For those you answered incorrectly, read the explanation carefully and see if you can find where you went wrong. Keep in mind that there will be more information about answering questions and reading passages in the chapters that follow.

Passage One

The Rainout

1   "This isn't fair mom!" I protested.

2   "This isn't about fairness Billy. You know you're still grounded," my mother replied.

3   I was the only one out of my group of friends who wasn't allowed to go to the Yankees game. This infuriated me so much that I stomped up the stairs and slammed my bedroom door shut. So what if I was still being punished for the low grade I received in math on my report card! Everyone was going, and I *was* working harder. I have actually been doing my homework and studying. After all, my last test grade in the class was a B. Couldn't my mother see that I was trying? Either she couldn't see that, or maybe if she did, she didn't care. I've tried to tell her that I've learned my lesson, but she never,

ever listens to me. I felt like a caged bird. I was only allowed out of the house to go to school, and then had to come straight home.

4   The clock reached 5:30, the time my friends were all meeting at Mark's house in order to carpool to the stadium. Each minute that passed by made my teeth clench tighter and tighter. How could this be happening to me?

5   Then, all of a sudden, through the open window in my room, I felt a strong breeze. A moment later I got a whiff of a familiar odor; the scent of the first few raindrops at the beginning of a rainstorm. I dashed to the window just in time to see the downpour. Then, a lightning bolt streaked across the sky. It was followed by a loud "Boom!" I was so startled that I jumped up and bumped my head on the windowsill. At that point reality hit me. The game would probably be rained out! I wasn't going to miss it! There would also probably be a make-up game. That game might take place after my grounding was over. As I thought about it, my jaw relaxed and even began to form a smile. I figured I should go and review my math homework, just to make sure I was ready for the next game!

Answer the following questions about the passage you just read:

1. The phrase in paragraph 3 of the passage, "like a caged bird," is an example of

   ○ A. a metaphor
   ○ B. a simile
   ○ C. personification
   ○ D. imagery

2. We can **infer** that the loud "Boom!" in the story was caused by

   ○ A. a tree that fell
   ○ B. the window slamming
   ○ C. the rain
   ○ D. thunder

3. In paragraph 3, what does the word **infuriated** mean?

   ○ A. angered
   ○ B. excited
   ○ C. saddened
   ○ D. upset

4. This passage is written from which perspective?

    ○ A. first person

    ○ B. second person

    ○ C. third person

    ○ D. fourth person

5. Which of the following is a conflict in the story?

    ○ A. Billy does not like when it rains.

    ○ B. Billy's mother is mean.

    ○ C. Billy cannot go to the game because of his poor grade.

    ○ D. Billy cannot play baseball.

6. Read the sentence from paragraph 3 of the passage.

> *I've tried to tell her that I've learned my lesson, but she never, ever listens to me.*

This sentence is an example of

    ○ A. a hyperbole

    ○ B. personification

    ○ C. a metaphor

    ○ D. a simile

7. What was an effect of the rainstorm?

    ○ A. Billy became angry.

    ○ B. Billy began to smile.

    ○ C. Billy's friends did not go to the game.

    ○ D. Billy was no longer grounded.

8. Which of the following describes the plot of the story?

    ○ A. The main character is upset about being grounded, complains to his mother about not being able to go to a baseball game, and then she decides to let him go.

    ○ B. The main character is upset about being grounded, complains to his mother about not being able to go to a baseball game, and then a storm gives him another chance to go to the game.

    ⊙ C. The main character is upset about being grounded and not being allowed to go to a baseball game, storms up to his room, and watches the game on television.

    ○ D. The main character wants to go to a baseball game with his friends, but it is rained out and he is disappointed.

9. Which of the following describes the theme of this story?

    ○ A. People must accept the consequences for their actions.
    ○ B. You can get your way if you yell enough.
    ○ C. Rain storms make you feel better.
    ○ D. Parents are unfair.

10. In the passage, the author used the rain to symbolize

    ○ A. unfairness
    ○ B. anger
    ○ C. baseball
    ○ D. opportunity

Passage Two

Babysitting

1   "Make sure Matty doesn't get into trouble while I'm gone," Jamie's mother said.

2   "I know, I know. I've done this a million times before," Jamie answered.

3   As she watched her mother walk through the door, Jamie realized that she had another long night of babysitting ahead of her. Her stare then turned toward her four-year-old brother who had a sneaky grin on his face. This grin usually meant he was up to something.

4   Just then, her brother darted up the stairs as fast as a cheetah. Jamie ran after him. She had trouble keeping up. He was lightning racing across the top floor of the house. By the time she caught up to him, she noticed he had something in his hand. It was a small piece of construction paper with a red heart on it. He handed the heart to Jamie. Even though there was no writing on it, she knew that the card said that her brother loved her. She could tell by the smile on his chubby little face. That smile made Matty's heart sing. Jamie then realized that the night might not be so bad. But she was still glad Matty wasn't twins!

Answer the following questions about the passage you just read:

1. Which statement from the passage is an example of personification?

O A. "But she was still glad Matty wasn't twins!" (paragraph 4)
O B. "As she watched her mother walk through the door . . ." (paragraph 3)
O C. "That smile made my heart sing." (paragraph 4)
O D. "She could tell by the smile on his chubby little face." (paragraph 4)

2. The part of the passage that says, "He was lightning racing across the top floor" (paragraph 4), is an example of

- ○ A. personification
- ○ B. a metaphor
- ○ C. a simile
- ○ D. a hyperbole

3. The purpose of using the simile, "like a cheetah" (paragraph 4), is to

- ○ A. tell how Matty climbs up the stairs
- ○ B. describe how quickly Matty moves
- ○ C. show why Matty left the room
- ○ D. show what kind of character Matty is

4. Which statement from the passage is an example of a hyperbole?

- ○ A. "I've done this a million times before." (paragraph 2)
- ○ B. "Jamie then realized that the night might not be so bad." (paragraph 4)
- ○ C. "But she was still glad Matty wasn't twins!" (paragraph 4)
- ○ D. ". . . Jamie realized that she had another long night of babysitting ahead of her." (paragraph 3)

5. This story is written from which point of view?

- ○ A. first person
- ○ B. second person
- ○ C. third person
- ○ D. none of the above

Answers

The Rainout

1. **B** Similes compare two things using the word *like* or *as*. The phrase uses the word *like* to compare Billy and a caged bird.

2. **D** We can infer that the sound is thunder because it follows lightning, just as thunder usually does.

3. **A** After becoming infuriated, Billy stomped up the stairs and slammed the door shut. This is something a person who is angry would do, so infuriated must mean angered.

4. **A** Billy is telling us the story. When the main character tells the story and refers to himself by using the word *I*, then the story is written in first person. An example of this can be found in the following sentence: "'This isn't fair mom!' I protested."

5. **C** The conflict of the story is that Billy wants to go to the game, but cannot because he is grounded because of his poor grade.

6. **A** Billy says that his mother never listens to him. This is an exaggeration, therefore it is an example of a hyperbole.

7. **B** As soon as Billy saw that it was raining, he realized the game would probably be rained out and then began to smile. He did not get angry. The passage doesn't state whether his friends went to the game or if he was no longer grounded.

8. **B** These are the main parts of the story in the correct order.

9. **A** Billy had to accept being grounded for his low grade. There were consequences to his actions, namely being grounded and not being able to go to the game. This is something the reader can learn from the story as well.

10. **D** Since it rained on the day of the game, it would probably be postponed and rescheduled to another day. Billy might then have the opportunity to go to that game if it was after he was no longer grounded. Therefore, the rain symbolized opportunity.

Babysitting

1. **C** This statement is the only one that has an object acting like a human. In this case, Matty's heart sings. The other sentences involve only a human character.

2. **B** The statement is not an exaggeration for effect, so D is incorrect. Plus it is talking about a human; therefore, answer A is incorrect. The statement is making a comparison between the brother and lightning. There is no use of *like* or *as*, so it cannot be a simile. Therefore, the statement is an example of a metaphor.

3. **B** This simile compares Matty and a cheetah, an animal that moves very quickly. It helps us to understand how Matty moves. Therefore, answers C and D are not correct, since they are talking about something else. Answers A and B both concentrate on Matty's movements. Only B concentrates on how quickly he moves, and that is why B is correct.

4. **A** Chances are Jamie didn't actually baby-sit a million times before. She says this to demonstrate to her mother that she has done this many times already, and is annoyed that her mother is telling her information that she already knows from babysitting before.

5. **C** The author is telling the story. The only time the reader sees the word *I* used is when a character is speaking and the word *I* is part of a sentence in quotation marks.

PARCC Multiple-Choice Questions

Typical multiple-choice questions usually follow a certain format. This format consists of the question, followed by three to five possible answers. Usually there is only one correct answer. The format on the PARCC is a bit different. For this type of multiple-choice question, or as it is also known, the Evidence-Based Constructed Response (EBCR), there is still a question followed by many possible answers. However, there are some differences. First, the question always has two parts, Part A and Part B. In addition, questions **may** have more than one answer. The question may ask something like this: "Which two answers, when added together, **best** support your answer to Part A?" It is important to read all parts of the question carefully so that you know how to answer them correctly.

Now you will have the opportunity to read two more passages. These passages will be followed by EBCR questions that are similar to those you will find on the PARCC. Read each passage and answer the questions that follow. Once again, the correct answers and explanations can be found at the end of this section. Make sure you check your answers.

Passage One

The Notebook

1   "Someone stole my notebook!" I yelled out in the middle of class. My comment startled not only the other students but our teacher, Mr. Klein, as well. I didn't mean for it to come out that way, but when I realized my notebook was missing, the words just rushed out of my mouth before I could stop them. Not only did my notebook contain all of my notes for English class, but my personal journal entries for the class, too. Since I didn't want anyone to read them, my notebook was with me at all times. It was never out of my sight. Now it was missing. No, someone had stolen it! How could this have happened?

2   I was snapped back to reality by Mr. Klein's stern comment, "Was yelling out really necessary, Ms. Martinez?" He always referred to us by our last names when he was upset with something we had done. I knew I was in trouble, but I had a really good reason for my behavior. Mr. Klein had to know that my outburst was just a simple reaction to the dreadful event that had occurred.

3   As I was pleading my case to Mr. Klein, I had an insight into what must have happened, and it hit me like a ton of bricks. It had to be Josephine! Yes, Josephine took, no stole, my journal. She'd been dying to get her grubby little hands on it ever since she heard that I wrote something bad about her in it. She confronted me about this about a week ago. I tried to explain to her that I never wrote about her in the journal. The truth is I had plenty of better things to write about. Josephine was not listening and kept saying that she would find out the truth, no matter what. She was the one who took my journal, and now there was no telling what she would do with it.

4   After English class, and on the way to lunch, I explained to my friends what had happened. I didn't know how I was going to do it, but I was going to confront Josephine and make her give back my notebook. I needed a plan. I pulled all of us into the girls' room for some privacy.

5   "Do you have any ideas?" I asked my friends. It was the first time all of us were silent. They all just shrugged their shoulders and shook their heads. Obviously I was going to have to be the one who was the mastermind and create the plan myself.

6   Suddenly, it was like a lightbulb turned on in my brain. I turned to the others and shouted, "I've got it!" The girls all stared at me and concentrated on every word I said. "Rosa, you will go over to Josephine when she is at her locker and ask her for notebook paper. She will have to go through her locker to pull out her notebook to get the paper. While she is doing that, Janeece, you peek in her locker to check to see if my notebook is in there. You know what my notebook looks like, right?"

7   "Sure, it's pink with white dots on it," Janeece replied.

8   "Great," I added, "I will be waiting around the corner. When you see my notebook, nod your head. When you give me that sign, I will run over and grab it from her locker. I will catch her red-handed!"

9 We walked out of the bathroom and into the hallway lined with rows of lockers. Just then we saw Josephine walking toward hers. I ducked around the corner. The plan went into action. It all happened so fast. Before I knew it, I saw Janeece nod her head. I ran out and yelled, "Gotcha!" I then grabbed the pink notebook sticking out of Josephine's locker.

10 Josephine replied, "What are you doing?"

11 "You stole my notebook, and I'm taking it back," I answered.

12 Just then I looked down at the notebook and realized it wasn't mine. It was pink, but had yellow dots on it. Janeece must have seen only that it was pink and thought it was mine. I didn't know what to say. All of a sudden I heard my name being yelled from down the hall. It was my friend Patty.

13 "Hi, Maria!" Patty said excitedly, "I have been looking for you everywhere. You dropped this in the hall this morning."

14 She handed me my pink notebook with white dots. I was so happy to have it, but then I realized what I had done to Josephine. After that, Josephine gave me an annoyed look, shook her head, and walked away. It was then I knew I had some apologizing to do.

15 I said to my friends, "Can you help me come up with a new plan to apologize to Josephine?" They all groaned and walked away. Some people just don't like planning, I guess.

1. Part A

What kind of person is Maria?

○ A. mean
○ B. quiet
○ C. strong-minded
○ D. insecure

Part B

Which of the following supports your answer to Part A?

○ A. "I didn't know how I was going to do it, but I was going to confront Josephine and make her give back my notebook." (paragraph 4)
○ B. "I knew I was in trouble, but I had a really good reason for my behavior." (paragrah 2)
○ C. "I will catch her red-handed!" (paragraph 8)
○ D. "All of a sudden I heard my name being yelled from down the hall." (paragraph 12)

2. Part A

Which statement **best** describes the conflict of the story?

○ A. The main character has a fight with another character in the story.
○ B. The main character must develop a plan to get her missing notebook back.
○ C. The main character's friends do not want to help her find her notebook.
○ D. The main character is missing her notebook, which is filled with important information.

Part B

Which sentence from the passage **best** supports your answer to Part A?

○ A. "It was then I knew I had some apologizing to do." (paragraph 14)
○ B. "I needed a plan." (paragraph 4)
○ C. "Mr. Klein had to know that my outburst was just a simple reaction to the dreadful event that had occurred." (paragraph 2)
○ D. "I didn't mean for it to come out that way, but when I realized my notebook was missing, the words just rushed out of my mouth before I could stop them." (paragraph 1)

3. Part A

The protagonist in the story is

- ○ A. Maria
- ○ B. Janeece
- ○ C. Patty
- ○ D. Josephine

Part B

Which detail from the story supports your answer to Part A?

- ○ A. "I then grabbed the pink notebook sticking out of Josephine's locker." (paragraph 9)
- ○ B. "It was never out of my sight. Now it was missing." (paragraph 1)
- ○ C. Some people just don't like planning, I guess. (paragraph 15)
- ○ D. "I didn't know what to say." (paragraph 12)

4. Part A

How is the conflict resolved?

- ○ A. Maria apologizes to Josephine.
- ○ B. Josephine admits stealing the notebook.
- ○ C. Maria finds the notebook hidden in Josephine's locker.
- ○ D. Patty tells Maria she found her notebook and hands it back to her.

Part B

Which detail **best** supports your answer to Part A?

- ○ A. "Can you help me come up with a new plan to apologize to Josephine?" (paragraph 15)
- ○ B. "They all groaned and walked away." (paragraph 15)
- ○ C. "You dropped this in the hall this morning." (paragraph 13)
- ○ D. "After that, Josephine gave me an annoyed look, shook her head, and walked away." (paragraph 14)

5. Part A

Which of the following can be this story's theme?

- ○ A. Keep your notebook close to you.
- ○ B. Making plans is fun.
- ○ C. It is not good to assume.
- ○ D. Teachers like when students yell in class.

Part B

Which of the following **best** supports your answer to Part A?

- ○ A. "She was the one who took my journal, and now there was no telling what she would do with it." (paragraph 3)
- ○ B. "Not only did my notebook contain all of my notes for English class, but my personal journal entries for the class, too." (paragraph 1)
- ○ C. "My comment startled not only the other students but our teacher, Mr. Klein, as well." (paragraph 1)
- ○ D. "Since I didn't want anyone to read them, my notebook was with me at all times." (paragraph 1)

Passage Two

Ach-oo!

1   Are you constantly sneezing, coughing, or getting a tissue to blow your nose? If you are, then you may be suffering from seasonal allergies. Seasonal allergies can also be known as hay fever. The most common symptoms are sneezing, itchy nose, itchy or sore throat, nasal congestion, runny nose, and coughing. These symptoms are often misdiagnosed as a cold. However, if they occur around the same time each year, then they could be signs that someone is suffering from seasonal allergies.

2   Seasonal allergies are caused by outdoor molds that release their spores and by trees, grasses, and weeds that release pollen. These are called allergens. If a person's body is allergic to these allergens, it will release chemicals to fight against them. The release of these chemicals causes the allergy symptoms. People may be allergic to the spores, pollen, or even both. In the northeastern part of the country, for example, certain types of pollen can be released as early as February. Other types of pollen or spores can be released any time from early spring through October. These are the most common times that people will experience allergy symptoms.

3   Some people also suffer from other symptoms that are related to seasonal allergies. They may develop wheezing and shortness of breath. This may mean that their allergies have developed into asthma. Another commonly related symptom is dark circles under the eyes. This is usually caused by the nasal congestion that is brought on by seasonal allergies.

4   There is no cure for allergies, but there are several ways to alleviate symptoms. First, there are preventative measures to reduce the contact a person has with allergens. These include keeping windows closed, using air conditioning when the weather gets warmer, and staying inside when pollen counts are high. If symptoms still persist, over-the-counter medications are an option.

5   However, these medications do not work for everyone. It may be necessary to see a special doctor who can properly diagnose seasonal allergies. This is done by exposing the skin to an allergen. If there is a reaction to the allergen, along with typical symptoms of seasonal allergies, then a diagnosis will be made. Once someone is diagnosed with seasonal allergies, he or she can be properly treated. There are many types of medications that can be prescribed to ease the symptoms. If symptoms are still present, then a person may require allergy shots to help find relief. Different people require different treatments, but the goal is always the same, to relieve them of their suffering from seasonal allergy symptoms.

1. Part A

In paragraph 4, the word **alleviate** most nearly means

- ○ A. increase
- ○ B. ease
- ○ C. change
- ○ D. correct

Part B

Which sentence from the passage supports your answer to Part A?

- ○ A. ". . . caused by the nasal congestion that is brought on by seasonal allergies." (paragraph 3)
- ○ B. "If symptoms still persist, over-the-counter medications are an option." (paragraph 4)
- ○ C. "First, there are preventative measures to reduce the contact a person has with allergens." (paragraph 4)
- ○ D. ". . . keeping windows closed . . ." (paragraph 4)

2. Part A

The purpose of the second paragraph is to

○ A. describe the symptoms of seasonal allergies
○ B. explain why trees release pollen
○ C. explain the causes of allergies
○ D. tell when allergy symptoms occur

Part B

Which detail from the text **best** supports your answer to Part A?

○ A. "Seasonal allergies are caused by . . ." (paragraph 2)
○ B. "These are the most common times . . ." (paragraph 2)
○ C. "Other types of pollen or spores can be released . . ." (paragraph 2)
○ D. ". . . it will release chemicals to fight against them." (paragraph 2)

3. Part A

We can **infer** from the passage that

○ A. people in the Northeast will not usually have allergy symptoms
   in December
○ B. people never have allergy symptoms in the winter
○ C. everyone is allergic to trees and molds
○ D. pollen affects everyone

Part B

Which **two** details from the passage, when combined, support your answer to
Part A?

☐ A. "The release of these chemicals causes the allergy symptoms."
   (paragraph 2)
☐ B. "Other types of pollen or spores can be released any time from early
   spring through October." (paragraph 2)
☐ C. "People may be allergic to the spores, pollen, or even both."
   (paragraph 2)
☐ D. "Some people also suffer from other symptoms that are related to
   seasonal allergies." (paragraph 3)
☐ E. ". . . certain types of pollen can be released as early as February."
   (paragraph 2)

4. Part A

According to the passage, what causes allergy symptoms?

○ A. chemicals the body releases
○ B. trees
○ C. air conditioning
○ D. open windows

Part B

Which **two** details from the passage support your answer to Part A?

☐ A. "The release of these chemicals causes the allergy symptoms." (paragraph 2)
☐ B. ". . . staying inside when pollen counts are high." (paragraph 4)
☐ C. "The most common symptoms are sneezing . . ." (paragraph 1)
☐ D. ". . . molds that release their spores and by trees, grasses, and weeds that release pollen." (paragraph 2)
☐ E. "If a person's body is allergic to these allergens . . ." (paragraph 2)

Passage Three

Read the passage taken from "Wilderness 2.0: Understanding How People Experience and Value Wilderness" (*www.naturalinquirer.org*). Answer the questions that follow.

1   When Congress passed the Wilderness Act of 1964, nearly every member of the Congress voted in favor of the act. The law, created by the passage of the act, permanently protects some of the most natural and undisturbed places in America. The act is one of the most successful U.S. environmental laws. It continues to be the guiding piece of legislation for all wilderness areas.

2   President Lyndon Johnson signed the Wilderness Act into law on September 3, 1964. Following the establishment of the Wilderness Act, other countries around the world have also protected natural areas. Few of these other areas worldwide, however, have the same level of protection from human activities as American wilderness areas.

Section 2(c) of the Wilderness Act of 1964 describes wilderness as follows:

3   A wilderness, in contrast with those areas where man and his own works dominate the landscape, is hereby recognized as an area where the earth and its community of life are untrammeled by man, where man himself is a visitor who does not remain. An area of wilderness is further defined to mean in this Act an area of undeveloped Federal land retaining its primeval character and influence, without permanent improvements or human habitation, which is protected and managed so as to preserve its natural conditions; and which (1) generally appears to have been affected primarily by the forces of nature, with the imprint of man's work substantially unnoticeable; (2) has outstanding opportunities for solitude or a primitive and unconfined type of recreation; (3) has at least five thousand acres of land or is of sufficient size as to make practicable its preservation and use in an unimpaired condition; and (4) may also contain ecological, geological, or other features of scientific, educational, scenic, or historical value.

4   Howard Zahniser (zah(n) ī zər), author of the Wilderness Act of 1964, selected the word "untrammeled" to define wilderness. Many people read the word "untrammeled" as "untrampled," as in not stepped on. Yet the word "untrammeled" means something much different. A "trammel" is a net used for catching fish, or a device used to keep horses from walking. To trammel something is to catch or restrain it. Untrammeled means something is free or unrestrained. Wilderness areas, therefore, are not to be controlled by humans. Zahniser defined "untrammeled" in the Wilderness Act.

5   **Wilderness Fun Facts**

- When the Wilderness Act of 1964 was passed, it protected 9.1 million acres of wilderness in 13 States.
- On the 50th anniversary of the Wilderness Act, the act now protects 109,511,966 acres of wilderness in 44 States and Puerto Rico.
- The smallest wilderness is Pelican Island Wilderness in northern Florida.
- This wilderness contains 5.5 acres of land and water.
- The largest wilderness is Wrangell-Saint Elias Wilderness in Alaska.
- This wilderness contains 9,078,675 acres.
- Only Connecticut, Delaware, Iowa, Kansas, Maryland, and Rhode Island have no designated wilderness areas.
- The newest wilderness area is Sleeping Bear Dunes in Michigan.
- It became an official wilderness area on March 13, 2014.

1. **Part A**

   What is the meaning of **legislation** as it is used in paragraph 1?

   ○ A. law
   ○ B. protection
   ○ C. document
   ○ D. environment

   Part B

   Which detail supports your answer to Part A?

   ○ A. "Few of these other areas worldwide, however, have the same level of protection from human activities . . ." (paragraph 2)
   ○ B. "President Lyndon Johnson signed the Wilderness Act into law . . ." (paragraph 2)
   ○ C. "The act is one of the most successful U.S. environmental laws." (paragraph 1)
   ○ D. ". . . other countries around the world have also protected natural areas." (paragraph 2)

2. **Part A**

   What is the **main** idea of the passage?

   ○ A. The Wilderness Act of 1964 was established to protect wilderness areas in the United States.
   ○ B. Howard Zahniser was the author of the Wilderness Act of 1964.
   ○ C. More areas are protected under the Wilderness Act now than in 1964.
   ○ D. Untrammeled means something unrestricted.

   Part B

   Which detail from the passage supports your answer to Part A?

   ○ A. "On the 50th anniversary of the Wilderness Act, the act now protects 109,511,966 acres of wilderness in 44 States and Puerto Rico." (paragraph 5)
   ○ B. "The law, created by the passage of the act, permanently protects some of the most natural and undisturbed places in America." (paragraph 1)
   ○ C. "Howard Zahniser (zah(n) ī zər), author of the Wilderness Act of 1964, selected the word 'untrammeled' to define wilderness." (paragraph 4)
   ○ D. "Untrammeled means something is free or unrestrained." (paragraph 4)

3. **Part A**

Why does the author of the passage include the fact that nearly every member of Congress voted in favor of the act?

- ○ A. The author wanted to prove how popular the act was.
- ○ B. The author wanted to demonstrate how Congress could agree.
- ○ C. The author wanted to show how important the act was.
- ○ D. The author wanted to show what happened in history on September 3, 1964.

Part B

Which detail supports your answer to Part A?

- ○ A. ". . . permanently protects some of the most natural and undisturbed places in America." (paragraph 1)
- ○ B. "President Lyndon Johnson signed the Wilderness Act into law on September 3, 1964." (paragraph 2)
- ○ C. "It continues to be the guiding piece of legislation for all wilderness areas." (paragraph 1)
- ○ D. Following the establishment of the Wilderness Act, other countries around the world have also protected natural areas." (paragraph 2)

4. **Part A**

What is the purpose of the passage?

- ○ A. to show how other countries do not care about wilderness areas
- ○ B. to inform the reader of the Wilderness Act of 1964 and how it affects wilderness land in the United States
- ○ C. to prove that Howard Zahniser was a very educated man
- ○ D. to show how old the act is

Part B

Which detail supports your answer to Part A?

- ○ A. "Zahniser defined 'untrammeled' in the Wilderness Act." (paragraph 4)
- ○ B. "Few of these other areas worldwide, however, have the same level of protection from human activities as American wilderness areas." (paragraph 2)
- ○ C. "The law, created by the passage of the act, permanently protects some of the most natural and undisturbed places in America." (paragraph 1)
- ○ D. ". . . other countries around the world have also protected natural areas." (paragraph 2)

5. Drag **four** of the details from the list to the box in **chronological** order to make a summary of the passage. (In this case, write the details in the box in chronological order.)

(1) "Only Connecticut, Delaware, Iowa, Kansas, Maryland, and Rhode Island have no designated wilderness areas." (paragraph 5)

(2) "It continues to be the guiding piece of legislation for all wilderness areas." (paragraph 1)

(3) "The law, created by the passage of the act, permanently protects some of the most natural and undisturbed places in America." (paragraph 1)

(4) "President Lyndon Johnson signed the Wilderness Act into law on September 3, 1964." (paragraph 2)

(5) "Many people read the word 'untrammeled' as 'untrampled,' as in not stepped on." (paragraph 4)

(6) "Following the establishment of the Wilderness Act, other countries around the world have also protected natural areas." (paragraph 2)

(7) "Few of these other areas worldwide, however, have the same level of protection from human activities as American wilderness areas." (paragraph 2)

6. Part A

Why is it important for wilderness areas not to be controlled by humans?

○ A. so that the animals can be free
○ B. to preserve the original state of the land
○ C. so they can be developed at a later time
○ D. so other countries can realize their beauty

Part B

Which detail supports your answer to Part A?

○ A. ". . . protected and managed so as to preserve its natural conditions . . ." (paragraph 3)
○ B. ". . . has at least five thousand acres of land or is of sufficient size as to make practicable its preservation . . ." (paragraph 3)
○ C. "Few of these other areas worldwide, however, have the same level of protection . . ." (paragraph 2)
○ D. ". . . may also contain ecological, geological, or other features of scientific, educational, scenic, or historical value." (paragraph 3)

Answers

The Notebook

1. **Part A: C; Part B: A**   Maria yells out in class and gets her friends involved in her plan. This shows that she is not quiet. Maria, the main character, is determined to get her notebook back and gets her friends involved in helping her. Another word for *determined* is *strong-minded*, and that is why **C** is the correct answer.

2. **Part A: D; Part B: D**   The problem the main character faces is that she cannot find her notebook. Answers A and C did not occur in the story. The main character's friends did want to help her find the notebook, and she did not have a fight with another character in this story. Answer B is incorrect because it is not a problem the character faces in the story; instead it is an event that happened in the story.

3. **Part A: A; Part B: B**   The protagonist is the character who must solve a problem. Maria is the one that has a problem in the story. Janeece and Patty are Maria's friends. Josephine is the character that Maria blames for taking her notebook.

4. **Part A: D; Part B: C**   Maria's problem is solved when Patty gives her back her notebook, and then tells Maria that she must have dropped it in the hallway.

5. **Part A: C; Part B: A**   Readers can learn from Maria that assuming can cause problems. Maria assumed that Josephine stole her notebook because of something Josephine had said earlier. Maria was proven to be wrong and then knew she had to apologize to Josephine for what she did.

Ach-oo!

1. **Part A: B; Part B: C** There is no cure for allergies, but there are things that a person can do (preventative measures) to alleviate or ease the symptoms.

2. **Part A: C; Part B: A** The entire paragraph explains the causes of allergies.

3. **Part A: A; Part B: B and E** The passage states that the most common time pollen or spores, which can cause allergy reactions, are released is from early spring through October. In the Northeast, certain types of pollen can even be released in February. Therefore, people in the Northeast will not usually experience seasonal allergies in December since pollen is not released at that time.

4. **Part A: A; Part B: A and E** If a person's body is allergic to allergens, then it will release chemicals to fight against them. These chemicals cause allergy symptoms.

Wilderness 2.0: Understanding How People Experience and Value Wilderness

1. **Part A: A; Part B: C** The Wilderness Act is a guiding piece of legislation, or law.

2. **Part A: A; Part B: B** The main idea of this passage is the Wilderness Act. The other statements are details that are in the passage but are not what the whole passage is about.

3. **Part A: C; Part B: C** The author wanted to show how important this act was. It was so important that it still guides the laws for all wilderness protection today.

4. **Part A: B; Part B: C** The purpose of the passage is to inform the reader of the act and what it does.

3. **3, 2, 4, 6** These are the most important details of the passage in chronological order.

4. **Part A: B; Part B: A** It is important for wilderness areas not to be controlled by humans so they can be preserved as they originally were.

The Narrative Writing Task

The Narrative Writing Task involves reading a story, answering questions, and writing your own, original narrative based on what you have read. A narrative is a story. It can be fiction (not true) or nonfiction (a true story). This part of the assessment can be easy for some students, but not so easy for others. Imagine this: You are given a passage to read. You come to the end only to realize you have no idea what you have just read. You realize this is because you were thinking about the party you are going to this weekend or the sports practice you have after school. Does this sound familiar? It happens to many students. Usually if this happens in class, you can reread the passage and go on from there. However, if you daydream during this part of the PARCC test, you may not have time to read the story again. Not only do you have to focus on the story, but you will also need to understand what the questions are asking. It's okay though, because by the time you finish this chapter you will be prepared with tips to help you stay focused. You will also have practiced many of the types of questions you will see on the test.

In this chapter you will

- learn about the parts of a narrative: character, plot, and language;
- practice writing a quality narrative;
- learn about the rubric; and
- review a sample narrative.

Character

There are two types of main **characters** in a story. First, there is the **protagonist**. This is the character in the story who has a problem and needs to solve it. The other type is the **antagonist**: the character who creates the problem for the protagonist.

Here is an example of each type of character from the fable "The Three Little Pigs":

Protagonist	The pigs are the protagonists because they face the problem of getting their houses blown down and must try to stop it from happening.
Antagonist	The antagonist is the wolf who is causing a problem for the pigs by trying to blow their houses down.

Point of View

The story is usually written from a certain **point of view**. The person or character telling the story determines the point of view, also known as the perspective. The two types most commonly used are **first person** and **third person**. In a first-person narrative, the narrator or main character is telling the story to the reader. You can easily tell if a passage is written in the first person because the words **I**, **me**, **us**, and **we** will be used often. The character explains how he or she feels as the story is being told. Third person is used when the author tells the story. The only time you will see the words **I**, **me**, **us**, and **we** is if a character is speaking, and the words will be in quotation marks.

Plot

The **plot** of a story is what actually happens in the story. If you took all of the events that happened in a story and put them together in order, they would create the plot. The elements of a plot are setting, conflict, climax, resolution, and theme.

The **setting** of the story is not only *where* the story takes place, but also *when* the story takes place, like the time of day or time of year. The setting can affect the **mood**, or feeling, readers get as they read the story. If you read a scary story, when and where does it usually take place? It's usually somewhere dark and quiet. This setting gets the audience ready to be scared by the monster that's ready to attack. This is exactly what the writer wants. If the setting were somewhere else, the audience might not be scared. For example, a story set in a haunted house during a thunderstorm will give the reader a different feeling than one that takes place in a park during a sunny day.

The **conflict** is the problem the main character(s) is faced with and must try to overcome. The conflict can be **external**, which means the problem exists outside or apart from the character. This can be another character, some other creature, or even the environment. A conflict can also be **internal**. These conflicts exist within the character, who may need to make a big decision or choose between right and wrong.

External conflict	A prince must get through a dangerous blizzard to rescue a princess. The conflict is between the prince and the blizzard.
Internal conflict	A character is invited to a party and wants to go, but the character's best friend is not invited. The character debates whether going to the party and possibly hurting the best friend's feelings is worth the fun of attending the party. In this case, the conflict is deciding whether or not to go to the party.

After the story begins, there are events that build **suspense** (the feeling that you can't wait to find out what is going to happen). These events are called the **rising action** of the story. In our story example, this would be where the wolf blows down the straw and stick houses. The rising action leads to the climax. The **climax** of a story is where protagonists begin to have their problem solved. It is often the most exciting part of the story. The climax of "The Three Little Pigs" is when the wolf tries to blow down the brick house containing the pigs, but is unable to do so. Next comes the **falling action**. This happens after climax has occurred and the conflict has been resolved. In our story, the falling action would be when the wolf climbs in the chimney and falls into the cauldron. Finally, there is the **resolution**. This is the conclusion of the story. Once again, in "The Three Little Pigs," the resolution is when the wolf runs off and leaves the pigs alone.

The **theme** of a story is the message the author is trying to send to the reader or the lesson learned from reading the story. From reading "The Three Little Pigs," we can learn that intelligence can sometimes be more important than strength. The last little pig was smart enough to build his house out of bricks. The wolf's strong exhale was no match for the bricks, and the wolf was defeated. Stories can sometimes have more than one theme.

Language

Sensory Language and Symbols

Often writers use **sensory language** to give the reader a better idea of what is happening in the story. Sensory language describes details that are "sensed" by the characters, what they see, hear, touch, taste, or smell. Writers also use **symbols** in their writing. Symbols are objects that represent ideas like love, anger, fear, good, or evil. For example, the wolf in "The Three Little Pigs" can symbolize wickedness.

Figurative Language

Figurative language is used by writers to help the reader picture what is going on in the story. This type of writing should not be taken literally. In other words, the words have a different meaning from what they actually say. For example, "her face was as red as a cherry." Does this mean that the girl's skin actually turned bright red? No, it has another meaning. We might say that someone's face turns red because she is blushing and her cheeks are flushed. This could be because the character is angry or embarrassed. Here is another example: "The old house seemed to say, 'Stay out!'"

This doesn't mean that the house really spoke. The sentence has another meaning. Can you take a guess as to what it really means? The author of this sentence means that the way the house looked from the outside gave us the feeling that it was old, abandoned, and did not want visitors.

There are several types of figurative language. This type of writing will very likely show up on a PARCC assessment. Make sure that you are familiar with it, by reviewing the most common types of figurative language:

- **Simile:** A simile is a comparison of two things. When comparing these two things, the words *like* or *as* are used. For example, "He was as big **as** a bear." This is a simile comparing the man and the bear. The comparison used the word *as*. This is definitely a simile, but what does it mean? It means that the man is very big. When we think of a bear, we think of a very big animal. Therefore, the man must be very big if we are comparing him to a bear.

- **Metaphor:** A metaphor is also a comparison but one in which you replace one thing with another. A metaphor will often use linking words such as *is*, *was*, or *are*. For example, "The man is a bear when it comes to getting his way." This metaphor tells us that the man is determined, just as a bear can be determined.

- **Personification:** Personification gives human traits to a nonhuman character. Here's an example: "The refreshing lake summoned me on the hot day." Does the writer literally mean that the lake called for the person? If not, then what does this statement mean? It means that the person was very hot and the refreshing lake was very appealing. This is an example of personification because the lake isn't human but the writer has given it the ability to call out or appeal to someone.

- **Hyperbole:** A hyperbole is an extreme exaggeration the writer uses to create an effect in the story. "I had about one million pages to read for homework last night," is a hyperbole. It doesn't mean that the character literally had one million pages to read. Instead, the writer wants the reader to understand that the character is complaining about doing the homework and exaggerating to prove that there was a lot to do.

Writing a Quality Narrative

You've read about the elements of a narrative, but how do you write one? The first thing you should do is to make sure that you understand what you are asked to write. Your story will be based on a passage that you've just read. You may be instructed to continue the story, write the same story but from a different character's perspective, or even change the ending of the story. Make sure you reread the question and make notes if necessary so that you know what you have to do. Once you know what you have to write about, take some time to **brainstorm** ideas. You can make a story web or just list ideas that come in to your mind. Take a few minutes to do this. When you finish, you will probably have more ideas than you need. Choose your best ideas that make the most sense. Once you are finished brainstorming and organizing your ideas, you can begin writing. Some tips to remember as you write your story are included in the table below.

Tip	Explanation
• Begin with a hook.	You want to begin your story in such a way that the reader will be interested from the beginning. There are several possible ways to begin. Here are two examples: • Use dialogue between characters. • Begin with three interesting adjectives to describe a main character or the setting. (Example: Hot, sticky, and smothering was the air on this August morning.)
• Include compositional risks. (Only include them if you are sure you are using them correctly.)	Examples of compositional risks are: • using figurative language • dialogue • complex sentences
• Make sure that you use the same type of writing style as the author of the story.	If the author used a lot of dialogue, make sure you include dialogue in your story. If the author used a lot of description, make sure you do too.

Tip	Explanation
• Make sure that you are writing a story that is based on the given task. Don't go off topic.	If you are asked to write a continuation of the story, make sure you begin where the passage in the assessment ends. If you are asked to write from another character's perspective, remember that this character may have seen different things, speak a certain way, or have different opinions. It should not be the same exact story as the one you read.
• Include conflict in the story.	Any good story has a conflict. Your story should be no exception. Remember to include the conflict and a resolution in your story.
• Make sure your story has a good beginning, middle, and end.	Your story should be interesting throughout. In order to do this, include great descriptions, details, and a good ending. You don't want to bore your reader and you definitely don't want to disappoint the reader with a rushed or dull ending.
• Remember proper grammar, mechanics, and sentence structure.	Try your best to include end marks where they belong, commas if you need them, and correct spelling. Also, if your story takes place in the past, use past tense verbs (*jumped, ran, went*). If it takes place in the present, use present tense verbs (*jump, run, go*). Try to avoid using both. This can confuse the reader.

Understanding the Rubric

Your essay will be scored using the Narrative Writing Task rubric located in Appendix A at the end of this book. The rubric ranges from 0 to 4 points in *Written Expression* and *Knowledge of Language and Conventions*. Written expression means your ability to include narrative elements in your response, develop a cohesive (organized) piece, and use an effective style. The better you are at fulfilling these requirements, the more likely you will be to score a 4 (the highest score in this section) in the written expression section.

For the knowledge of language and conventions section, you must demonstrate your understanding of mechanics (spelling, punctuation, capitalization), grammar, and usage. The fewer mistakes in grammar, mechanics, or usage, the higher your score will be. In this case, the highest score you could receive is a 3.

Sample Narrative

Now that you have read about narratives, it is time to read one and respond to questions. Try your best and don't worry; answers and a brief explanation follow each question.

Read the narrative below and answer the questions that follow.

This is an excerpt (part of the story) from "The Seven Ravens," by Maura McHugh.

1   There was once a couple who had seven sons, and as much as they loved their boys, they often wished for a daughter. One day, while driving cattle through a field, the husband found a copper ring in the middle of a circle of red-capped mushrooms and decided it must be lucky. Holding it in his palm, he made a wish for a daughter and then gave the ring to his wife, telling her it was charmed.

2   Soon after, his wife became pregnant and the entire household waited for the arrival of the new child with great excitement. To everyone's delight, a girl was born, but the labor had been long and difficult, and the baby girl—whom they named Una—was sickly and unwell. A house full of boys is rarely quiet, but during this time they all spoke in hushed tones and hung about the house, hoping Una would get better. All of them wanted to do something to help.

3   Finally, their father decided to set them a task to get them out from under his feet. He gathered all the boys and instructed the oldest to take their pewter pitcher and fill it with water from the stream that flowed through the field in which he had discovered the ring. He explained that the water had healing properties that could save his sister.

4   Upon hearing this all the boys clamored to go and created a loud fuss. Their father pretended to accede to their demands, and asked them to complete the task together. The boys raced to the river, each of them eager to be the one who would save their sister. But they fell to arguing over who would draw water from the stream. Soon all of them were grabbing at the pitcher. A tugging match ensued, and in the struggle the pitcher tumbled into the river with a splash and disappeared.

5   The boys were silent for a time. Their parents didn't have much money, and the pitcher was a favorite of their father's. They squabbled amongst themselves over who was to blame, but they were really putting off returning home and reporting their failure to their father. They had nothing else in which to carry the water home.

6   The day wore into evening, and back home the boys' father became impatient. He was caring for his wife, who was still worn out from childbirth, and watching over his frail baby girl. He imagined that the boys were out playing instead of completing the simple chore he had given them.

7   He decided to place the ring under Una's pillow in the hope that it would effect a cure. While it was in his hand he looked out of the window and saw ravens swooping in the sky. He frowned and gripped the ring hard. "I wish those foolish sons of mine were all turned into ravens!" he declared.

8   In that moment there was a rushing of wings and seven black ravens flew past the window.

9   The boys never returned home. The husband and wife were distraught, but during the long months of futile searches their little girl was a comfort to them. Una recovered and thrived but she grew up thinking she was an only child, for her parents were careful never to mention her brothers.

1. **Part A**

What is the meaning of **clamored** as it is used in paragraph 4?

○ A. to speak noisily
○ B. to speak calmly
○ C. to remain silent
○ D. to take turns

Part B

Which part of the sentence from the story supports the answer to Part A?

○ A. ". . . asked them to complete the task together." (paragraph 4)
○ B. ". . . raced to the river . . ." (paragraph 4)
○ C. ". . . created a loud fuss." (paragraph 4)
○ D. ". . . all of them were grabbing . . ." (paragraph 4)

2. Which of the following details would be important to include in a summary of the story? Drag the details to the boxes in chronological order. (In this case, write one detail on the lines provided in **chronological** order.)

(A) "To everyone's delight, a girl was born, but the labor had been long and difficult, and the baby girl—whom they named Una—was sickly." (paragraph 2)

(B) "Holding it in his palm, he made a wish for a daughter and then gave the ring to his wife, telling her it was charmed." (paragraph 1)

(C) "The day wore into evening, and back home the boys' father became impatient." (paragraph 6)

(D) "A tugging match ensued, and in the struggle the pitcher tumbled into the river with a splash and disappeared." (paragraph 4)

(E) "The boys were silent for a time." (paragraph 5)

(F) "He frowned and gripped the ring hard." (paragraph 7)

(G) "'I wish those foolish sons of mine were all turned into ravens!' he declared." (paragraph 7)

1. --

2. --

3. --

4. --

3. Part A

In the story, how did the father's attitude change toward his sons?

- ○ A. At first he was furious, but then he became sad.
- ○ B. At first he was sad, but then he became overjoyed.
- ○ C. At first he was doubtful, but then he became trusting.
- ○ D. At first he was loving, but then he became furious.

Part B

Which **two** details from the story support the answer to Part A?

- ☐ A. "The boys never returned home." (paragraph 9)
- ☐ B. "Their father pretended to accede to their demands and asked them to complete the task together." (paragraph 4)
- ☐ C. "He frowned and gripped the ring hard." (paragraph 7)
- ☐ D. "I wish those foolish sons of mine were all turned into ravens!" (paragraph 7)
- ☐ E. "He was caring for his wife, who was still worn out from childbirth, and watching over his frail baby girl." (paragraph 6)

4. In the story "The Seven Ravens," the seven brothers are turned into ravens as a result of a wish that their father made. Write an original story about the brothers trying to get back to see their sister. Use what you have learned about their characters as you tell what happens next.

BRAINSTORM HERE

Write your story response here:

Answers to "The Seven Ravens"

1. **Part A: A; Part B: C** We know that *clamored* means to speak noisily because the boys clamored and created a loud fuss when they wanted to go. They were not being quiet or calm and they did not take turns.

2. **The summary details in chronological order are: B, A, D, G** These details are a necessary part of the summary. Without one of them, a reader would not know generally what happened in the story. The other details support the story, but are not necessary in the summary.

3. **Part A: D; Part B: B and D** These statements show how the father began as loving, where he trusted his sons to help their sister, and changed to being furious, where he wished that his sons were changed into ravens as punishment.

4. Following is a sample response to the same question from "The Seven Ravens."

Brainstorming:

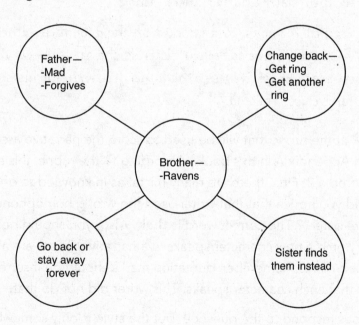

Sample Response

"We have to get back to see if our sister is ok," said the oldest brother. "What if Dad yells at us and tells us to leave again?" said the youngest brother. "We have to try!" said another brother.

So all of the brothers flew back to the house to see there sister. But then they realized that they were ravens. "How could we change back into boys? said one brother. "We have to get the ring from Dad. If we hold it and wish that we were boys again it might work.

So the oldest brother flew into the house as the father was cleaning the ring. He grabbed the ring from his father and held it in his beak. And then he flew out the door. Just as they decided they would make a wish to be boys again as they held the ring. It worked! They ran over to a mirror and saw there face. They all jumped for joy! So they decided that they would make the trip back to the house to see their sister and face there father.

When they reached the house and knocked on the door their father answered it. "Father we have come home to see our sister. Is she ok? We know that we were foolish and just beg your forgiveness." The father felt sorry for his sons. Your sister is ok. I forgive you. The end.

Let's take a look at the rubric that will be used to score the narrative assessment. (It can be found in Appendix A in this book.) According to the rubric, this sample would probably be scored a 2. First, there are many mistakes in knowledge of language and conventions. Did you notice that that writer used the wrong homophone in "*there* face" and "*there* sister"? The correct word is **their**. Also, you should begin a new paragraph every time a new character speaks in a narrative. There are also some missing quotation marks. Remember, quotation marks should be inserted before and after the words that each character speaks. This writer did not do that.

The writer does respond to the question, but the style is only somewhat effective. It is always best to include details from the story in your response. In addition, sentence beginnings should vary. This helps to keep the reader interested. Did you notice how many times the writer began a sentence with the word **so** or another conjunction like **but** or **and**? It's best to avoid using these words as the first word in a sentence. Next, was there any description in the sample response? Description helps the reader to picture what the writer is saying. Description helps keep the reader interested. This narrative lacked details and description. And finally, what did you think about the ending? It is not necessary to write "The End" after you finish. If you don't rush the ending, your reader will know it is the end. There will be no wondering about it. To sum up, using details, description, varied sentence beginnings, and a good ending will improve your story and help your written expression.

Now, let's see a revised and edited version of the same response.

"We have to get back to see if our sister is ok," said the oldest brother.

"What if Dad yells at us and tells us to leave again?" said the youngest brother.

"We have to try!" said another brother.

Immediately all of the brothers flew back to the house to see their sister. But then they realized that they were ravens. "How could we change back into boys?" said one brother.

"We have to get the ring from Dad. If we hold it and wish that we were boys again it might work."

So the oldest brother flew into the house just as the father was cleaning the enchanted copper ring. He grabbed it from his father and held it in his beak. Then he flew out the door as quickly as possible and returned to his brothers. They made a wish to be boys again as they held the ring. They could then feel themselves changing. Their wings turned to arms and their claws changed back into feet. It worked! They raced over to a mirror and saw their faces. No beaks! No feathers! They all jumped for joy!

They decided that they would make the trip back to the house to see their sister and face their father. When they reached the house and knocked on the door their father answered it. Seeing them he slammed the door shut again. The boys were disappointed but did not want to give up. The oldest brother then yelled through the door, "Father we have come home to see our sister. Is she ok? We know that we were foolish and just beg your forgiveness." The father felt sorry for his sons. Slowly the brothers saw the door creak open.

"Your sister is well. I forgive you," said their father with a tear in his eye.

At that moment the brothers knew they would be a family once again.

Even though this response is not perfect, it is more detailed and many of the errors in language and conventions have been corrected. It is now more interesting and easier to read.

A Side-by-Side Comparison of the Two Responses	
First Response	Revised Response
More than one character speaks in a paragraph.	There is a new paragraph each time a new character speaks.
There are spelling mistakes.	The correct *their* is used.
Missing punctuation marks	Quotation marks are placed around all of the words each character speaks.
There is not much detail. For example, "The father was cleaning the ring."	Details from the story are added, plus more description is included. "The father cleaned the enchanted copper ring." This makes the response more descriptive and interesting.
The ending is rushed. The father quickly forgives his sons.	The ending has more detail. The door creaks open, showing the father's hesitation, but still his forgiveness.

The Literary Analysis Task

This part of the assessment deals with reading different types of passages and analyzing them. Analyzing means to read and examine something closely, understand it, and then be able to answer questions about it. You may also be given a map, chart, or graph to examine. To analyze a passage, you need to understand the arrangement of the paragraphs in passages or the structure of the paragraph, what the author is trying to say in the passage, and *why* the author is saying it.

There are two types of reading passages: fiction and nonfiction. As you may know, fiction stories are ones that aren't true. They can be fantasy stories that include talking animals or creatures from another planet or realistic stories that haven't actually happened. On the other hand, nonfiction passages are ones that are true. Often they are about a historical person or event. You may see either or both of these types of passages on this section of the test.

In this chapter you will

- read about main ideas, details, purpose, and vocabulary;
- learn about relationships in passages;
- review the rubric for this assessment; and
- review some sample passages.

Main Idea, Details, and Purpose

Nonfiction passages have a central thought that they are trying to explain to the reader. This central thought is called the **main idea**. The main idea is what the paragraph or passage is mostly about. It usually can be found at the beginning of the paragraph, but is not always found there. To have a full paragraph, the writer needs to add more information or **details**, about the main idea. Details tell more about the main idea and give you a better understanding of what you are reading.

The author of the passage often has a **purpose**, or reason, for writing about a topic. The purpose may be to tell you how the author feels about a topic. The way the author lets you know how he or she feels about a topic is called the **tone**. For example, if the author likes a topic, then he or she will probably use positive adjectives in the writing. If the author is opposing the topic, then there will most likely be negative adjectives in the writing.

Another purpose for writing can be to **persuade** the reader to feel a certain way about a subject. To persuade means to try to get the reader to think the way the author thinks. The author usually doesn't state his or her feelings openly. Instead, the reader gets a sense of how the author feels by certain things that are said in the paragraph. For example, consider the following sentence: "The marvelous creature stood on top of the hill looking down at its prey." How do you think the author feels about the creature in the sentence? Chances are the author likes the creature because even though the creature is about to attack its prey, the author still calls it *marvelous*, another word for wonderful. The author is using a complimentary tone. The author doesn't have to say that he or she likes the creature. The readers know this by the words the writer chooses to describe the creature.

Vocabulary

Vocabulary is important in all types of writing. Have you ever read a book or passage and come to a word that you didn't know? Your first instinct may be to skip the word and continue reading, but then you may lose the meaning of the paragraph. Instead, you may decide to look it up in a dictionary, ask a friend what it means, or ask your teacher to help you. When you're taking the PARCC test, however, you cannot do any of these things. Does that mean that you should just skip over the word and hope for the best? That may not be the best idea for two reasons. First, you may lose the meaning of the paragraph. Second, there may be a multiple-choice question that asks you to define this word. Not to worry. There are context clues to help you.

Context clues are words or sentences near the word you don't know that can help you to understand what the confusing word means. For example, "The pie was so delectable that I couldn't wait for a second helping." You may not know what the word *delectable* means, but if you read the sentence carefully you can figure it out. The pie was delectable, and a pie is something you usually eat. If you want some more of something, it must mean that it tastes good; therefore, delectable must mean that something tastes good. Using context clues can mean the difference between understanding a paragraph and being stuck on a word.

Relationships in Passages

The PARCC assessment may include multiple-choice or other types of questions that ask you about the relationships in a passage. These relationships are compare-contrast, cause-effect, and being able to infer. **Comparing** is telling how two ideas are alike. **Contrasting** is telling how those same two ideas are different. For instance, compare and contrast the wolf in "Little Red Riding Hood" and the wolf in "The Three Little Pigs." One example of a comparison is that both wolves are alike because they tried to eat innocent characters in the story. However, they are different because one wolf did not try to hide himself, while the other disguised himself as Little Red's grandmother. You may be able to come up with many examples, but the important thing is to think about the relationship based on what the question is asking.

In a cause-and-effect relationship, the **cause** not only comes before the effect, but also makes it happen. The **effect** is the result. Think about taking a test. If someone does not study for a test, what is probably going to happen? The student will probably not do well, right? Well, the cause is not studying and the effect is not doing well on the test. Not studying can *cause* you to do poorly on a test.

Inferring requires you to draw a conclusion about something in a passage based on the information that the author has provided. Basically, the reader has to make an educated guess about something in the passage. For example, in the statement "Gina and Rosita are best friends and in the same class," if Rosita is in sixth grade, what can we **infer** about Gina? We are told that the girls are in the same grade. We also know that Rosita is in sixth grade. Based on these two facts, we can infer that Gina is in the sixth grade also. We are not told this specifically, but we can take a pretty good guess based on what we know.

An additional skill you may be required to demonstrate is being able to tell fact from opinion. A **fact** is something that is true and can be proven. An **opinion** is what someone believes about a topic. A fact is that George Washington was the first president of the United States. We can prove this statement by looking it up in a history textbook or an encyclopedia. An opinion is that George Washington was the best president. There is no absolute proof of this, and other people may say that another president was the best. Be careful because authors often try to make their opinions sound like facts, especially when they are trying to persuade you to agree with them.

In addition to reading and answering questions based on one passage, you will be asked to read another passage and answer questions for that reading. Then, you will be asked to write an essay in which you will probably have to compare or contrast the two pieces. Remember to read the question carefully so that you know exactly what to do.

Before you can begin writing, you will need to brainstorm and organize your ideas. Some tips to remember as you begin your response are included in the table below.

Tip	Explanation
• Begin with brainstorming.	If you are asked to write a response that compares and contrasts two passages, you can list the similarities and differences or use a Venn diagram.
• Use details from the passage to support your writing.	When you say something is similar to or different from something else, you should state an example or direct quote from the passage to prove that you are correct.
• In a compare-and-contrast response, you should remember to state both.	State how the two things or people are alike and how they are different.
• Remember proper grammar, mechanics, and sentence structure.	Try your best to include end marks where they belong, commas if you need them, and correct spelling. Also use proper capitalization.
• Use transition words to show comparisons and contrasts.	Examples of transition words that compare: *also, and, similarly* Examples of transition words that contrast: *however, conversely, on the other hand*

Writing the Essay

After brainstorming ideas, it's time to write your analysis. Your essay should be at least three paragraphs, but it will most likely be four or five. You should include an introduction, one body paragraph to tell about the first passage, one body paragraph to tell about the second passage, and then a concluding paragraph to sum up your ideas.

Your introduction should include the names and authors of both passages. It should also include a sentence or two about each passage. This should be followed by your **thesis**, or response to the question.

A body paragraph should include the name of the passage. It should also include your full explanation of how this passage relates to the question. For example, if the question asks how the author developed the theme, this is where you should tell how the author lets the reader know what the theme is. Did the author reveal the theme through a character's actions? Did the author reveal the theme through a character's words or thoughts? Make sure that you fully explain your ideas and also include examples from the text to prove that your ideas are correct. It is also a good idea to set up a quote from the text by first saying something like, "In the text it states . . ." or even, "According to the text . . ." This lets the reader know that you have direct proof from the passage to support your response. Make sure that you explain everything thoroughly so that the reader is not expected to try to read your mind.

The conclusion should once again include both titles and your thesis statement. It should also recap the most important details from your essay. No new information should be included in this paragraph. The final sentence should be a wrap-up about both passages.

Understanding the Rubric

The rubric that will be used to assess your literary analysis essay is located in Appendix B at the end of this book. This rubric will also be used to evaluate your research simulation essay.

The first section of the rubric is *Reading Comprehension of Key Ideas and Details*. This section examines how well you showed that you were able to understand and analyze what you read, and also support this analysis with evidence from the text. The highest score in this area is a 4.

The second section assesses *Written Expression*. Here, the rubric evaluates the essay for effective style and progression of ideas. It also includes a section that assesses how well you develop your ideas and support them with evidence from the text. The last section of the rubric, *Knowledge of Language and Conventions*, is the same as for the narrative writing task. The highest score you can receive in this section is a 4.

Sample Passages

Now it's time for you to read, analyze, and answer questions. Read the following passage and then respond to the questions that follow. You will see the answer and a brief explanation after each question.

Read the passage below and answer the corresponding questions.

This passage is taken from *Albert Einstein and the Theory of Relativity*, by Robert Cwiklik.

1   People the world over had opened their arms and their hearts to Albert and Elsa, but on their return to Germany, the Einsteins received a very different reception. Many Germans still felt bitter and humiliated by their recent defeat in World War I. Germany was still reeling from the loss of the vast amounts of money spent trying to fund the huge war effort. Now, money was tight, and people were growing desperate and uneasy. They wanted someone to blame for their problems.

2   Some Germans felt that the country had been weakened by people who had not supported the war—pacifists, intellectuals, and Jews especially. Albert was all of these things, and he became the focus of the frustration that his countrymen were now feeling. In Berlin, large public meetings were held

to denounce Albert and his theories. Ignorant men claimed that no Jewish person could ever arrive at a true physical theory; only "Aryan" German minds could think like that. Albert's theories were labeled, contemptuously, "Jewish physics."

3   Albert realized the attacks on him and his work were ignorant and unfounded. The best scientific minds in the world had tested his theories and approved them, but that didn't stop the critics. They called meeting after meeting to denounce Albert. There were even rumors that Albert's life was in danger, that he would be assassinated to avenge Germany's honor, which he supposedly had tarnished. This was surely twisted thinking, for Albert had brought honor to Germany in his travels to all corners of the globe.

4   Albert chose not to hide from his tormentors. One evening, a large anti-Einstein rally was held in Berlin. Speaker after speaker led the large crowd of spectators in vicious attacks on Albert's theories and character. In the midst of this hateful scene, a new spectator shuffled into the hall and took a seat near the front. The crowd instantly recognized the shaggy-haired man sitting there as Albert Einstein himself.

5   As the speakers railed on and on with their ridiculous accusations, Albert sat back and laughed out loud. The more preposterous their claims, the louder he laughed. The people in the audience could not believe their eyes. How was it, they thought, that Albert dared to enter this lions' den of his enemies? No matter what they thought of him that night, many of the people in the audience could not help but admire Albert's courage. He had not allowed threats of assassination to stop him from getting a good laugh at his enemies' expense.

6   Albert did what he could to restore his country's faith in him. He even became a German citizen again, though he was later to regret it as "the biggest folly of my life." For, no matter what he did, many Germans would not give him peace. They needed a scapegoat to blame their failures on, and the peaceful physicist was an easy target.

7   Albert did not allow his critics to distract him from his work for long, however. Now that he had expanded his theory of relativity, he wished to work on another bothersome problem. He had always believed in the unity of

nature, which is why he felt that relativity must hold true for all motion, not just constant motion. Now, Albert felt that nature's unity must be understood by physics in a whole new way.

8   Quite properly, Einstein felt himself to be in the mainstream of physics. In the whole history of the subject, there had been a trend toward the unification of ideas. Faraday found the relationship between electricity and magnetism, and Maxwell brought light into the same picture. The relativity theories had united gravitation with acceleration and mass with energy. The author of these unifying ideas now set out to finish the job. He would find a "unified field theory." This was to be a complete theory of physics, joining the knowledge of gravitational and electromagnetic waves into a single theory. The subatomic world and the most distant reaches of the universe would be described in the same set of equations.

1. Part A

What was the effect of Albert Einstein attending the rally?

- ○ A. He gained admirers.
- ○ B. He was physically attacked.
- ○ C. He changed his thinking.
- ○ D. He left disappointed.

Part B

Drag **two** details from the story that support your answer to Part A into the box. (In this case, check off the two details that support your answer.)

- ☐ A. "He had not allowed threats of assassination to stop him . . ." (paragraph 5)
- ☐ B. "How was it, they thought, that Albert dared to enter this lions' den of enemies?" (paragraph 5)
- ☐ C. ". . . many people in the audience could not help but admire Albert's courage." (paragraph 5)
- ☐ D. "As the speakers went on and on with their ridiculous accusations, Albert sat back and laughed out loud." (paragraph 5)
- ☐ E. ". . . a new spectator shuffled into the hall and took a seat near the front." (paragraph 4)

2. Part A

What can we **infer** about Faraday and Maxwell?

- ○ A. They did not approve of Einstein's theories.
- ○ B. They were not at the rally.
- ○ C. They were in the crowd at the rally.
- ○ D. They were scientists.

Part B

Which **two** details, when put together, support your answer to Part A?

- ☐ A. "...Maxwell brought light into the same picture." (paragraph 8)
- ☐ B. "This was to be a complete theory of physics..." (paragraph 8)
- ☐ C. "Albert did not allow his critics to distract him from his work for long, however." (paragraph 7)
- ☐ D. "Now, Albert felt that nature's unity must be understood by physics in a whole new way." (paragraph 7)
- ☐ E. "Faraday found the relationship between electricity and magnetism..." (paragraph 7)

3. Part A

What does the word **spectators** mean as it is used in paragraph 4?

- ○ A. critics
- ○ B. viewers
- ○ C. conductors
- ○ D. supporters

Part B

Which detail from the story supports your answer to Part A?

- ○ A. "The crowd instantly recognized the shaggy-haired man sitting there as Albert Einstein himself." (paragraph 4)
- ○ B. "...shuffled into the hall and took a seat near the front." (paragraph 4)
- ○ C. "Speaker after speaker led the large crowd..." (paragraph 4)
- ○ D. "One evening, a large anti-Einstein rally was held in Berlin." (paragraph 4)

Now you will read an excerpt from, *Tim Tebow: A Promise Kept*, by Mike Klis, and then answer the questions that follow.

1   On March 26, 2012, Tim Tebow entered the New York Jets' indoor practice field facility in Florham Park, NJ, wearing a Jet-green tie, a well-tailored gray suit, a fashionable two-day stubble, and his ever-present grin.

2   "It's such an honor for me to be here," said Tebow, greeting the throng of New York press there to meet and question him. "I'm so excited about being a Jet."

3   To many, witnessing Tebow introduced as a new player with the New York Jets was unusual, if not startling. After his sensational career at the University of Florida, one of the best in college football history, Tebow was selected by the Denver Broncos in the first round of the 2010 NFL draft. Many football experts were surprised Tebow had been drafted that highly. They said Tebow would fail as a pro quarterback because of his seriously flawed passing motion.

4   Tebow's achievements in his first two seasons, particularly in 2011, proved his critics wrong. Tebow played well in his three-game audition to finish his rookie year with the Broncos. Still, the Broncos' new management team operations director John Elway and head coach John Fox were skeptical. A competition in training camp led to veteran Kyle Orton getting the starting quarterback job for the third consecutive season.

5   But by the end of the 2011 season, Tebow was not only playing, but playing so well that he became the most talked about player in the NFL. Tebow pulled out miracle win after miracle win with clutch, fourth quarter performances, often in the final minutes of the game. He led a Broncos team that was so bad, it had not reached the playoffs in six years. He led a Broncos team that was so bad, the year before, in 2010, it tied for the league's second-worst record. He led a Broncos team that was so bad in 2011, it started the season with a 1–4 record with Orton as the starter.

6 Yet, from the time Tebow became the Broncos' starting quarterback in Game 6 of the 2011 season, the team then won seven of its next eight games. That 7–1 run included a six-game winning streak that was enough to lift the Broncos to the AFC West Division title and had a playoff berth in the post-season.

7 In the playoffs, Tebow had arguably his best game as a pro, throwing for 316 yards to defeat the heavily favored Pittsburgh Steelers, 29–23 in overtime, at the Broncos' home of Sports Authority Field at Mile High. The winning score came on the first and the last play of overtime when Tebow threw a perfectly accurate pass to Demaryius Thomas down the middle of the field.

1. Part A

How do you think the author feels about Tim Tebow?

- ○ A. He feels Tim Tebow is overrated.
- ○ B. He feels Tim Tebow is a terrible quarterback.
- ○ C. He feels Tim Tebow needs to improve his football skills.
- ○ D. He feels Tim Tebow is a good quarterback.

Part B

Which detail supports your answer to Part A?

- ○ A. "To many, witnessing Tebow as a new player with the New York Jets was unusual, if not startling." (paragraph 3)
- ○ B. ". . . Tebow would fail as a pro quarterback . . ." (paragraph 3)
- ○ C. "By the end of the 2011 season, Tebow was not only playing, but playing so well that he became the most talked about player in the NFL." (paragraph 5)
- ○ D. ". . . experts were surprised Tebow was drafted that highly." (paragraph 3)

2. **Part A**

What does the word **skeptical** mean as it is used in paragraph 4?

○ A. positive
○ B. doubtful
○ C. convinced
○ D. neutral

Part B

Which details from the story support your answer to Part A?

○ A. "A competition in training camp led to veteran Kyle Orton getting the starting quarterback job . . ."
○ B. ". . . Tebow was selected by the Denver Broncos in the first round of the 2010 NFL draft."
○ C. ". . . proved his critics wrong."
○ D. "Tebow played well in his three-game audition . . ."

3. You read passages from *Tim Tebow: A Promise Kept* and *Albert Einstein: The Theory of Relativity*. The authors used the third-person point of view in both passages. Describe how the authors used this point of view to develop each of the characters. Use details from the passages to support your answer.

```
┌─────────────────────────────────────────────────────┐
│                   BRAINSTORM HERE                    │
│                                                       │
│                                                       │
│                                                       │
│                                                       │
│                                                       │
│                                                       │
│                                                       │
│                                                       │
│                                                       │
│                                                       │
└─────────────────────────────────────────────────────┘
```

Write your response here:

Answers

Albert Einstein and the Theory of Relativity

1. **Part A: A; Part B: B and C** Since Albert Einstein went to the rally, people realized it took a lot of courage to go where a person would be criticized and they admired him for that.

2. **Part A: D; Part B: A and E** We do not know if they were at the rally. The passage did not tell us that they did not approve of Einstein's theories. We know that light, magnetism, and electricity are studied by scientists. We were told that Faraday and Maxwell created theories in these areas. Therefore, Faraday and Maxwell must be scientists.

3. **Part A: B; Part B: C** The spectators were part of the crowd. Therefore, the spectators must be viewers watching the speakers.

Tim Tebow: A Promise Kept

1. **Part A: D; Part B: C** The author does talk about how others were not supportive of Tebow and his skills, but always reports Tebow's accomplishments on the field. This supports the fact that he thinks Tebow is a good quarterback.

2. **Part A: B; Part B: A** Even though Tim Tebow did well, the coaches were skeptical, or doubtful, especially when the veteran quarterback performed better in the competition.

3. Following is a sample brainstorming and response. Based on the rubric located in Appendix B, what would you score this response?

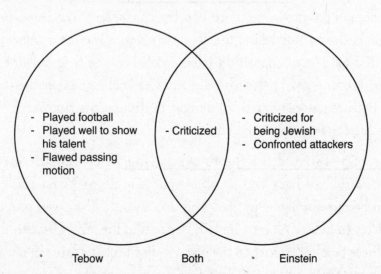

Sample Response

In the passage Albert Einstein and the Theory of Relativity by Robert Cwiklik and the passage Tim Tebow: A Promise Kept by Mike Klis, both authors used the third-person point of view to develop the characters. They used this point of view to develop the characters through the characters actions.

In Albert Einstein and the Theory of Relativity the author tells us about Albert by showing how he went to the anti-Einstein rally. "Einstein chose not to hide from his tormentors." Albert Einstein was brave to do this.

In Tim Tebow: A Promise Kept the author also tells us about Tim through his actions. "Tebow played well in his three-game audition to finish his rookie year with the Broncos." This shows that Tim was a good player.

In conclusion, the authors of both passages developed their characters through their actions. Albert Einstein went to a rally and confronted his tormentors. Tim Tebow played very well in his three-game audition. Both men were strong and brave.

This response would probably receive a score of 2. Although there weren't many mistakes in language or conventions, the quotes do not fully support the writer's response. In addition, there is not much of an explanation for the reader to fully understand what the writer is trying to say.

Now let's see a revised version of the same response.

In the passage Albert Einstein and the Theory of Relativity by Robert Cwiklik and the passage Tim Tebow: A Promise Kept by Mike Klis, both authors used third person point of view to develop the characters. The third-person point of view is the author telling the story through a narrator. Albert Einstein was a scientist who faced opposition from people because they did not like his religion. Tim Tebow faced critics who did not like how he passed the football. The authors of both passages used third person to develop the characters through the actions each man took in the story.

In Albert Einstein and the Theory of Relativity, Albert Einstein was not someone who would sit back and let others put him down. Many people were against him because he was a pacifist and was Jewish. They even had anti-Einstein rallies to attack Albert Einstein's scientific theories. Einstein did not hide from these people. He went to the rally. In the text it states in paragraph 5, "As the speakers railed on with their ridiculous accusations, Albert sat back and laughed out loud" (Cwiklik). The narrator of the story told us that Albert not only faced the tormentors, but also laughed at them. This lets the reader know that he was courageous to stand up to people attacking him and his theories.

In Tim Tebow: A Promise Kept, Tim Tebow is someone who would not let people who doubted him stop him from doing his best. Many thought he was not good enough to be a professional quarterback. He worked hard to prove them wrong. In paragraph 5 it states, "But by the end of the 2011 season, Tebow was not only playing, but playing so well that he became the most talked about player in the NFL" (Klis). This shows that Tebows actions proved to everyone that he was qualified for the job. He was confident enough to keep going even though many doubted him.

In conclusion, the authors of Albert Einston and the Theory of Relativity and Tim Tebow: A Promise Kept used the third-person point of view to develop their characters through the characters' actions. The narrator told us that Einstein went to a rally where people were attacking his theories. This showed his courage. The narrator told us that Tim Tebow did not let others tell him that he was not good enough to become a professional quarterback. This shows that he had confidence in himself. All in all, both men did not let others stop them from achieving their dreams.

This response includes more direct details from the story and additional explanations to support the writer's ideas. Although it contains some spelling and punctuation errors, it would receive a minimum score of 3

| A Side-by-Side Comparison of the Two Responses ||
First Response	Revised Response
There is no explanation of third-person point of view.	This point of view is explained in the introduction and throughout the essay.
Quotes are written with little explanation.	The writer set up the quotations from each passage by stating where they are located in the text and the author's name. There is also an explanation for how each quote supports the response.
Titles are not underlined.	These passages are excerpts from a book and should be underlined.

Here are two more passages to analyze. The first is an excerpt from *The Velveteen Rabbit* by Margery Williams. Read the passage and answer the questions that follow.

1   There was once a velveteen rabbit, and in the beginning he was really splendid. He was fat and bunchy, as a rabbit should be; his coat was spotted brown and white, he had real thread whiskers, and his ears were lined with pink sateen. On Christmas morning, when he sat wedged in the top of the Boy's stocking, with a sprig of holly between his paws, the effect was charming.

2   There were other things in the stocking, nuts and oranges and a toy engine, and chocolate almonds and a clockwork mouse, but the Rabbit was quite the best of all. For at least two hours the Boy loved him, and then Aunts and Uncles came to dinner, and there was a great rustling of tissue paper and unwrapping of parcels, and in the excitement of looking at all the new presents the Velveteen Rabbit was forgotten.

3   For a long time he lived in the toy cupboard or on the nursery floor, and no one thought very much about him. He was naturally shy, and being only made of velveteen, some of the more expensive toys quite snubbed him. The mechanical toys were very superior, and looked down upon everyone else; they were full of modern ideas, and pretended they were real. The model boat, who had lived through two seasons and lost most of his paint, caught the tone from them and never missed an opportunity of referring to his rigging in technical terms. The Rabbit could not claim to be a model of anything, for he didn't know that real rabbits existed; he thought they were all stuffed with sawdust like himself, and he understood that sawdust was quite out-of-date and should never be mentioned in modern circles. Even Timothy, the jointed wooden lion, who was made by the disabled soldiers, and should have had broader views, put on airs and pretended he was connected with Government. Between them all the poor little Rabbit was made to feel himself very insignificant and commonplace, and the only person who was kind to him at all was the Skin Horse.

4   The Skin Horse had lived longer in the nursery than any of the others. He was so old that his brown coat was bald in patches and showed the seams underneath, and most of the hairs in his tail had been pulled out to string bead necklaces. He was wise, for he had seen a long succession of mechanical toys arrive to boast and swagger, and by-and-by break their mainsprings and

pass away, and he knew that they were only toys, and would never turn into anything else. For nursery magic is very strange and wonderful, and only those playthings that are old and wise and experienced like the Skin Horse understand all about it.

5   "What is REAL?" asked the Rabbit one day, when they were lying side by side near the nursery fender, before Nana came to tidy the room. "Does it mean having things that buzz inside you and a stick-out handle?"

6   "Real isn't how you are made," said the Skin Horse. "It's a thing that happens to you. When a child loves you for a long, long time, not just to play with, but REALLY loves you, then you become Real."

7   "Does it hurt?" asked the Rabbit.

8   "Sometimes," said the Skin Horse, for he was always truthful. "When you are Real you don't mind being hurt."

9   "Does it happen all at once, like being wound up," he asked, "or bit by bit?"

10   "It doesn't happen all at once," said the Skin Horse. "You become. It takes a long time. That's why it doesn't happen often to people who break easily, or have sharp edges, or who have to be carefully kept. Generally, by the time you are Real, most of your hair has been loved off, and your eyes drop out and you get loose in the joints and very shabby. But these things don't matter at all, because once you are Real you can't be ugly, except to people who don't understand."

11   "I suppose *you* are real?" said the Rabbit. And then he wished he had not said it, for he thought the Skin Horse might be sensitive. But the Skin Horse only smiled.

12   "The Boy's Uncle made me Real," he said. "That was a great many years ago; but once you are Real you can't become unreal again. It lasts for always."

13   The Rabbit sighed. He thought it would be a long time before this magic called Real happened to him.

14   There was a person called Nana who ruled the nursery. Sometimes she took no notice of the playthings lying about, and sometimes, for no reason whatever, she went swooping about like a great wind and hustled them away

in cupboards. She called this "tidying up," and the playthings all hated it, especially the tin ones. The Rabbit didn't mind it so much, for wherever he was thrown he came down soft.

15   One evening, when the Boy was going to bed, he couldn't find the china dog that always slept with him. Nana was in a hurry, and it was too much trouble to hunt for china dogs at bedtime, so she simply looked about her, and seeing that the toy cupboard door stood open, she made a swoop.

16   "Here," she said, "take your old Bunny! He'll do to sleep with you!"

17   That night, and for many nights after, the Velveteen Rabbit slept in the Boy's bed.

18   And so time went on, and the little Rabbit was very happy—so happy that he never noticed how his beautiful velveteen fur was getting shabbier and shabbier, and his tail becoming unsewn, and all the pink rubbed off his nose where the Boy had kissed him.

19   Spring came, and they had long days in the garden, for wherever the Boy went the Rabbit went too. And once, when the Boy was called away suddenly to go out to tea, the Rabbit was left out on the lawn until long after dusk, and Nana had to come and look for him with the candle because the Boy couldn't go to sleep unless he was there. He was wet through with the dew and quite earthy from diving into the burrows the Boy had made for him in the flower bed, and Nana grumbled as she rubbed him off with a corner of her apron.

20   "You must have your old Bunny!" she said. "Fancy all that fuss for a toy!"

21   The Boy sat up in bed and stretched out his hands.

22   "Give me my Bunny!" he said. "You mustn't say that. He isn't a toy. He's REAL!"

23   When the little Rabbit heard that he was happy, for he knew that what the Skin Horse had said was true at last. The nursery magic had happened to him, and he was a toy no longer. He was Real. The Boy himself had said it.

24   That night he was almost too happy to sleep, and so much love stirred in his little sawdust heart that it almost burst. And into his boot-button eyes, that had long ago lost their polish, there came a look of wisdom and beauty, so

that even Nana noticed it next morning when she picked him up, and said, "I declare if that old Bunny hasn't got quite a knowing expression!"

25   That was a wonderful Summer!

1. Part A

What does the word **splendid** mean as it is used in paragraph 1?

- ○ A. ugly
- ○ B. average
- ○ C. marvelous
- ○ D. plain

Part B

Which detail from the story supports your answer to Part A?

- ○ A. ". . . Velveteen Rabbit was forgotten." (paragraph 2)
- ○ B. ". . . he had real thread whiskers, and his ears were lined with pink sateen." (paragraph 1)
- ○ C. "He was naturally shy . . ." (paragraph 3)
- ○ D. ". . . being only made of velveteen . . ." (paragraph 3)

2. Part A

What is an effect of a toy becoming Real?

- ○ A. It begins to fall apart.
- ○ B. It feels worried.
- ○ C. It is teased.
- ○ D. It is ignored.

Part B

Which detail from the story supports your answer to Part A?

- ○ A. ". . . the more expensive toys quite snubbed him." (paragraph 3)
- ○ B. ". . . the poor little Rabbit was made to feel himself very insignificant and commonplace . . ." (paragraph 3)
- ○ C. "The mechanical toys were very superior . . ." (paragraph 3)
- ○ D. ". . . most of your hair has been loved off, and your eyes drop out and you get loose in the joints and very shabby." (paragraph 10)

3. **Part A**

What made the rabbit think that the Skin Horse was Real?

- ○ A. The Skin Horse lived there a long time.
- ○ B. The Skin Horse was wise.
- ○ C. The Skin Horse knew how toys became Real.
- ○ D. The Skin Horse had parts that were worn out.

Part B

Which detail from the story supports your answer to Part A?

- ○ A. "The Skin Horse had lived longer in the nursery than any of the others." (paragraph 4)
- ○ B. "For nursery magic is very strange and wonderful . . ." (paragraph 4)
- ○ C. "He was so old that his brown coat was bald in patches and showed the seams underneath . . ." (paragraph 4)
- ○ D. "'Real isn't how you are made,' said the Skin Horse." (paragraph 6)

The second passage is an excerpt from *The Wonderful Wizard of Oz*, by Frank Baum. Once again, read the passage and answer the questions that follow.

1 "Good day," said the Scarecrow, in a rather husky voice.

2 "Did you speak?" asked the girl, in wonder.

3 "Certainly," answered the Scarecrow. "How do you do?"

4 "I'm pretty well, thank you," replied Dorothy politely. "How do you do?"

5 "I'm not feeling well," said the Scarecrow, with a smile, "for it is very tedious being perched up here night and day to scare away crows."

6 "Can't you get down?" asked Dorothy.

7 "No, for this pole is stuck up my back. If you will please take away the pole I shall be greatly obliged to you."

8 Dorothy reached up both arms and lifted the figure off the pole, for, being stuffed with straw, it was quite light.

9   "Thank you very much," said the Scarecrow, when he had been set down on the ground. "I feel like a new man."

10   Dorothy was puzzled at this, for it sounded queer to hear a stuffed man speak, and to see him bow and walk along beside her.

11   "Who are you?" asked the Scarecrow when he had stretched himself and yawned. "And where are you going?"

12   "My name is Dorothy," said the girl, "and I am going to the Emerald City, to ask the Great Oz to send me back to Kansas."

13   "Where is the Emerald City?" he inquired. "And who is Oz?"

14   "Why, don't you know?" she returned, in surprise.

15   "No, indeed. I don't know anything. You see, I am stuffed, so I have no brains at all," he answered sadly.

16   "Oh," said Dorothy, "I'm awfully sorry for you."

17   "Do you think," he asked, "if I go to the Emerald City with you, that Oz would give me some brains?"

18   "I cannot tell," she returned, "but you may come with me, if you like. If Oz will not give you any brains you will be no worse off than you are now."

19   "That is true," said the Scarecrow. "You see," he continued confidentially, "I don't mind my legs and arms and body being stuffed, because I cannot get hurt. If anyone treads on my toes or sticks a pin into me, it doesn't matter, for I can't feel it. But I do not want people to call me a fool, and if my head stays stuffed with straw instead of with brains, as yours is, how am I ever to know anything?"

20   "I understand how you feel," said the little girl, who was truly sorry for him. "If you will come with me I'll ask Oz to do all he can for you."

21   "Thank you," he answered gratefully.

22   They walked back to the road. Dorothy helped him over the fence, and they started along the path of yellow brick for the Emerald City.

23   Toto did not like this addition to the party at first. He smelled around the stuffed man as if he suspected there might be a nest of rats in the straw, and he often growled in an unfriendly way at the Scarecrow.

24   "Don't mind Toto," said Dorothy to her new friend. "He never bites."

25   "Oh, I'm not afraid," replied the Scarecrow. "He can't hurt the straw. Do let me carry that basket for you. I shall not mind it, for I can't get tired. I'll tell you a secret," he continued, as he walked along. "There is only one thing in the world I am afraid of."

26   "What is that?" asked Dorothy; "the Munchkin farmer who made you?"

27   "No," answered the Scarecrow; "it's a lighted match."

1. Part A

What is the meaning of **tedious**, as it is used in paragraph 5?

- A. boring
- B. exciting
- C. sickening
- D. interesting

Part B

Which detail from the story supports your answer to Part A?

- A. "I'm pretty well, thank you, . . ." (paragraph 4)
- B. ". . . perched up here night and day to scare away crows." (paragraph 5)
- C. "I feel like a new man." (paragraph 9)
- D. "I'm not feeling well," said the Scarecrow, with a smile, ..." (paragraph 5)

2. Read the list of central ideas and decide if each one can be found in *The Velveteen Rabbit, The Wonderful Wizard of Oz,* or both. Drag each idea to the proper box. (In this case, just write each idea in the correct box.)

Don't judge a book by its cover.

Sometimes you have to listen to those with more experience.

Don't worry about what others think.

Believe in yourself.

Have the courage to improve yourself.

The Velveteen Rabbit	Both	The Wonderful Wizard of Oz

3. You have read a passage from *The Velveteen Rabbit* and *The Wonderful Wizard of Oz*. Write an essay that identifies a similar theme in each text. Compare and contrast the approaches each text uses to develop this theme. Support your response with evidence from both texts.

BRAINSTORM HERE

Write your response here:

Answers

The Velveteen Rabbit

1. **Part A: C; Part B: B**   The passage states that the rabbit had real thread whiskers, was shaped just like a rabbit, and he had pink sateen ears. This supports the idea that the rabbit was really special, or marvelous.

2. **Part A: A; Part B: D**   The Skin Horse says that becoming real takes time and happens after a toy is used for a while. It does not happen for toys that are easily broken. Therefore, an effect of being real is that it begins to fall apart from all of the use.

3. **Part A: D; Part B: C**   The rabbit knew that being real caused a toy to become shabby. He noticed that the Skin Horse had parts that were worn, he was bald in patches, and was missing hair. The Skin Horse was shabby, so he must be real.

The Wonderful Wizard of Oz

1. **Part A: A; Part B: B**   The Scarecrow stated that he was perched night and day to scare away crows. He did the same thing all the time. Doing the same thing all the time can be boring, so *tedious* must mean boring.

2.

The Velveteen Rabbit	Both	The Wonderful Wizard of Oz
Don't judge a book by its cover.	Don't worry about what others think.	Have the courage to improve yourself.
Sometimes you have to listen to those with more experience.	Believe in yourself.	

3. Following is a sample brainstorming and response. Based on the rubric located in Appendix B, what would you score this response?

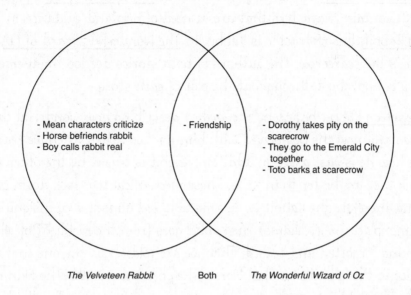

| The Velveteen Rabbit | Both | The Wonderful Wizard of Oz |

Sample Response

One theme that can be found in both passages is the importance of friendship. Both stories have characters that need help and had friends that do help them. In <u>The Velveteen Rabbit</u>, the rabbit needs help to become real. The skin horse becomes the Rabbit's friend and helps explain how to become real. The skin horse also helped the rabbit to understand that just because he wasn't fancy or mechanical, didn't mean he wasn't a good toy or couldn't be real. In fact, the skin horse was one of the only toys that was nice to the rabbit. The others made him feel like less of a toy since he was plain.

In The Wonderful Wizard of Oz, the scarecrow became friends with Dorothy and she offered to take him to see the wizard to get a brain. Just like the skin horse was willing to be a friend and help the rabbit, Dorothy was willing to be a friend and help the scarecrow.

This response would probably be scored a 2. There are a few mistakes in conventions, namely, many of the characters do not begin with a capital letter, as they do in each passage. More importantly, this essay was supposed to compare and contrast how each passage develops the theme. This response only speaks about how the approaches are similar, not how they are different. In addition, the response only refers to the passages, it does not contain specific evidence from both texts.

Now let's see a revised version of the same response.

The Velveteen Rabbit by Margery Williams and The Wizard of Oz by Frank Baum both contain characters that are in need of help and guidance. In The Velveteen Rabbit, this character is Rabbit. In The Wonderful Wizard of Oz, this character is the scarecrow. The authors of both stories develop the theme, friendship is important, throughout the plot of each story.

The Velveteen Rabbit begins by the author describing how wonderful the Rabbit was and how the boy played with him for two hours. Then we read on to see how he is cast aside. In addition, Rabbit is teased by the other toys that think they are better than he is. These mechanical toys look down on the Rabbit and therefore the Rabbit is, ". . . made to feel himself very insignificant and commonplace . . ." (Williams) The Rabbit goes from the highlight of all of the gifts to being forgotten and teased. Then we are told about the one character who is nice to the Rabbit, the Skin Horse. They become friends. The Skin Horse also guides the Rabbit to understand how to become Real. He takes the time to explain how a toy can become Real. Because he does this, the Rabbit knows when he is loved enough to become Real and really understands what this means. He is now no longer insignificant. This has a lot to do with his friendship with the Skin Horse.

The Scarecrow and Dorothy meet one another in the beginning of the passage from The Wonderful Wizard of Oz. This is unlike the Skin Horse and Velveteen Rabbit who became friends later in the text. Dorothy and the Scarecrow begin talking and Dorothy realizes quickly that the Scarecrow has a problem. That problem is that he is stuck on a pole. Dorothy immediately helps him off the pole. Dorothy then tells him that she is going to see Oz hoping that he can send her back to Kansas. She finds out that the Scarecrow has another problem. He has straw instead of a brain. The Scarecrow asked Dorothy if he could go with her to see Oz much like the Rabbit asked the Skin Horse to explain how to become Real. Right away she invites him along for the journey. Unlike the Skin Horse who had answers for the Rabbit, Dorothy didn't know if Oz could give the Scarecrow a brain. However, she said, "but you may come with me, if you like. If Oz will not give you any brains you will be no worse off than you are now." (Baum) She wanted to at least try to help the Scarecrow.

Both passages demonstrate the importance of friendship. They both showed how one character was willing to help another. However, in The Velveteen Rabbit, the Rabbit's problem was solved partly because of his friendship with the Skin Horse. In <u>The Wonderful Wizard of Oz</u>, although Dorothy did help the Scarecrow off of the pole, we don't know if she was able to help him receive a brain. But at least she tried.

In conclusion, the authors of <u>The Velveteen Rabbit</u> and <u>The Wonderful Wizard of Oz</u> develop the theme, friendship is important, throughout each story by the way one character helps another. However, in <u>The Velveteen Rabbit</u>, the Skin Horse helps the Velveteen Rabbit later in the plot and helps him to find the answer to his question. This is unlike <u>The Wonderful Wizard of Oz</u>, where Dorothy tries to help the Scarecrow from the beginning. She just doesn't have all the answers for him. The characters of both stories show us that kind actions are important to good friendships.

A Side-by-Side Comparison of the Two Responses	
First Response	Revised Response
Many of the main characters are not capitalized.	All main characters are capitalized. For example, the Scarecrow, the Skin Horse.
There are only comparisons of the two stories.	There are comparisons (both stories have characters who helped another character). There are also contrasts (The Skin Horse in *The Velveteen Rabbit* knows how to become Real and explains this to the Rabbit. However, in *The Wonderful Wizard of Oz*, Dorothy does not know if Oz can help the Scarecrow, but she invited him on the journey anyway.).
There are only references to both passages.	There are direct quotations from both passages that are used as textual evidence. - ". . . made to feel himself very insignificant and commonplace." -". . . but you may come with me, if you like. If Oz will not give you any brains you will be no worse off than you are now."

| A Side-by-Side Comparison of the Two Responses | |
First Response	Revised Response
There are very few, if any, transition words used.	Transition words are used to help the reader move from one part of the response to another. Words like: *however, in addition, then*
Only one of the Scarecrow's problems is mentioned.	Both problems are mentioned to show that Dorothy was willing to help the Scarecrow, even though she had just met him.

The Research Simulation Task

This part of the assessment will require you to view three informational sources. These sources may be in the form of passages, articles, blogs, charts, pictures, or a video. After examining what you have read or watched, you will be asked to analyze the information and then answer questions. You will also be required to write one analytical essay. In this essay you may be required to state your opinion on a topic and then provide evidence from the text to prove your opinion. This may be different from persuasive essays you have written in the past. This essay does include your opinion; however, you must prove your point by citing examples and statements from the passages. On the other hand, you may be asked to compare and contrast aspects, or properties, of the passages. Again, as you do this, remember to include evidence from passages or video. The evidence you provide is extremely important. This tells the person scoring your essay that you thoroughly understand what you have read and can also defend your answer. Simply giving an answer is not enough. You must prove why your answer is correct. In this section, and on the sample tests, you will be given two passages to read.

In this chapter you will

- read about sources for passages;
- get some tips on writing the essay; and
- review some sample passages.

The Sources

Chances are that you will be given two passages and one picture, video, or chart. It is a good idea to review the questions and essay before you read the passages so that you know what to focus on as you read. Remember, this is a timed assessment, so you have no time to waste by reading passages more often than you need to. Take notes on scrap paper as you read. You can use a Venn diagram, T-chart, or any other way of taking notes that works best for you. Since you will have three sources, it is best to take notes in a manner that can compare the information from all three sources easily. You can review all three sources on the computer by clicking on the tab for that source. You will see the tabs for each source once you have viewed all three.

Here are samples of a Venn diagram and T-chart graphic organizer:

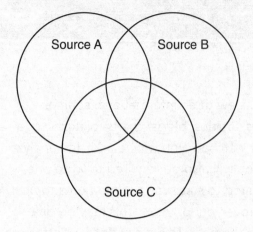

Source A	Source B	Source C

Venn Diagram for Three Sources   **T-Chart for Three Sources**

As you watch a video, it's easy to miss important information. Remember that you can rewind it and pause it so that you can take notes. It is also a good idea to write down the time in the video when something important is said so that you can fast forward to that part if you need to watch it again.

Writing the Essay

After you have reviewed all of the sources, make sure that you understand what the essay question is asking. Is it asking you to compare articles? Is it asking which article makes the strongest argument? Does the question want you to provide evidence from one, two, or all three sources? Double-check the question so you know how to respond with the best answer that will get you the highest score. After you are sure what the question is asking, look at your notes from the sources. It is important to then brainstorm for a few minutes to get some thoughts together. After all, you must not only state your opinion, but also provide evidence from the sources that will support your opinion, or **thesis**. You may even think about and include facts that you have already learned about the subject. As you brainstorm, organize your thoughts in a manner that will make it easy for you to include them in your essay. Organize them in the way that works best for you. Here is an example:

Thesis (Opinion):

_____

_____

	Source A Evidence	Source B Evidence	Source C Evidence
Reason 1 _____ _____			
Reason 2 _____ _____			
Reason 3 _____ _____			

After brainstorming, you are ready to begin writing your essay. Your essay should be *at least* three paragraphs. Most likely, it will be four or five paragraphs. Your essay should begin with an introduction and then state your thesis. The introduction should be interesting so that it hooks the reader's attention. Next, you will write the body of your essay. You should have two or three strong reasons to support your thesis. Each reason should be presented in a separate paragraph. As you are writing each body paragraph, you should not only state a reason, but clearly identify the supporting evidence including the source that provided the evidence. You can even state how another source had other information that is different or weaker than your supporting proof. If you are asked to analyze sources for their arguments, by demonstrating how another source is weaker, you are showing how your evidence is superior, thus making a stronger claim.

Your essay should end with a concluding paragraph. The concluding paragraph should begin by repeating your thesis. Don't word your thesis exactly as you did in your first paragraph. Rephrase it to get your point across once again. Then briefly state the reasons for your thesis again. Finally, end with a summarizing statement. No new information should be included in your conclusion.

Here are some tips for writing your essay:

Tips	Examples
Types of hooks to begin paragraph 1: • Ask a question of your reader. This should not be a yes/no question. Instead, it should make the reader think about the topic. • State an interesting bit of information about the topic. • Write three words describing your topic. • Have the reader think about something.	• How can zoos say they are protecting animals when they are preventing them from developing the natural instincts that will help them to survive? • Every minute of every day people are committing acts that are contributing to the demise of the environment. • Unjust, treacherous, and ungrateful are three words to describe how the colonists felt about the British government. • Imagine going to a school where everyone looks the same: the same clothes, the same colors, the same patterns.
When you write your thesis, do not use the word "I." The word "I" should be kept out of your entire essay. It makes your essay sound too personal.	Avoid: "I think the third source is the strongest." Instead use: "Source 3 makes the most compelling argument . . ."
Use transitions, or signal words, to move from one point in your essay to another. Some transition words are: *first of all, initially, then, in addition, next, in conclusion, in summary, to conclude*	• In conclusion, the colonists had every right to demand independence from the British. • In addition, source B states . . .
It is important to remember that your opinion is not enough in this essay. You must provide evidence from the sources to support your opinion.	

Tips	Examples
Make sure to not only state your evidence, but also tell which source provided the evidence.	
Remember that no new information should be included in your last paragraph.	
Remember to leave some time at the end to revise and edit your essay.	

Sample Passages

Now it's time for you to read, analyze, and answer questions. Read the following passage and then respond to the questions that follow. You will see the answers and a brief explanation after the questions.

The following is an excerpt from *Leonardo Da Vinci*, by Anthony Mason.

Court Painter

1   As court painter, part of Leonardo's job was to portray people from the court of Ludovico Sforza in Milan. Most of his portraits are of women, wives of rich and famous noblemen. They look young, beautiful, and serene. These portraits may be particularly idealized, but Leonardo also managed to capture the character of his different subjects.

True Portraits

2   In Milan, Leonardo developed more theories about painting. He believed that careful observation led to understanding, and that artists had an important role to play because they could record this understanding in precise and accurate images. He made many sketches of everything around him, particularly faces and parts of the body. He also observed the way that light fell on faces, fingers, hair, and clothes, revealing their structure. He applied what he had learned to his portraits. His use of light and shadow made the figures look solid and lifelike. The effect is called *chiaroscuro*, which means "light-dark" in Italian.

3   Another artist using such a delicate, smooth technique might have made the sitter look simply pretty and rather characterless. But in his portraits, Leonardo aimed to show not just what the sitters looked like, but their mental state as well—the sort of people they were.

Master of Portraiture

4   What distinguished Leonardo's painting was his ability to make everything look solid and three-dimensional. He managed this through close examination of shadow and careful use of color. In this, Leonardo was at least 50 years ahead of his time. Other painters were struggling with the same problem, but most of their work looks flat compared to his. Leonardo gives additional force to his portraits by using plain, dark backgrounds. These make the effect of light falling on the smooth skin of his sitters even more striking.

1. Part A

What is the meaning of the word **idealized** as it is used in paragraph 1?

- ○ A. glamorized
- ○ B. realized
- ○ C. painted
- ○ D. accurate

Part B

Which of the following details supports your answer to Part A?

- ○ A. "Most of his portraits are of women . . ." (paragraph 1)
- ○ B. ". . . but Leonardo also managed to capture the character of his different subjects." (paragraph 1)
- ○ C. ". . . part of Leonardo's job was to portray people from the court . . ." (paragraph 1)
- ○ D. "They look young, beautiful, and serene." (paragraph 1)

2. Part A

How does the author show that Leonardo Da Vinci believed that, "careful observation led to understanding . . ."?

- ○ A. by describing how Leonardo Da Vinci was 50 years ahead of his time
- ○ B. by describing how Leonardo Da Vinci developed more theories about painting
- ○ C. by describing how Leonardo Da Vinci used light and shadow
- ○ D. by describing how other painters were struggling with painting

Part B

Which detail from the passage supports your answer to Part A?

- ○ A. "In this, Leonardo was at least 50 years ahead of his time." (paragraph 4)
- ○ B. "He also observed the way that light fell on faces, fingers, hair, and clothes . . ." (paragraph 2)
- ○ C. ". . . artists had an important role to play . . ." (paragraph 2)
- ○ D. "Leonardo gives additional force to his portraits . . ." (paragraph 4)

3. Part A

What is the author's **main** purpose in *Leonardo Da Vinci*?

- ○ A. to explain how Leonardo Da Vinci became a distinguished painter
- ○ B. to describe Leonardo Da Vinci's painting techniques
- ○ C. to describe Leonardo Da Vinci's job as a court painter
- ○ D. to explain how Leonardo Da Vinci used *chiaroscuro*

Part B

Which **two** details below, when put together, support your answer to Part A?

- ☐ A. "He made many sketches of everything around him . . ." (paragraph 2)
- ☐ B. "He believed that careful observation led to understanding . . ." (paragraph 2)
- ☐ C. "His use of light and shadow made the figures look solid and lifelike." (paragraph 2)
- ☐ D. "The effect is called *chiaroscuro*, which means 'light-dark' in Italian." (paragraph 2)
- ☐ E. "In Milan, Leonardo developed more theories about painting." (paragraph 2)

The following is an excerpt from *Michelangelo and the Renaissance*, by David Spance.

1   Michelangelo's influence on the course of Western art and architecture has been profound. The challenge of drawing the naked human form in complicated poses persists as a test for the would-be artist even today.

2   The strength of Michelangelo's work lies in [the artist's] ability to understand, imitate, and even surpass the classical masters, and to build on this by following his own spirit of invention. By influencing Italian art he influenced European art, and thereby art of the Western world. His buildings still dominate Rome today, and his sculptures and paintings are monumental milestones in the course of the history of art. Michelangelo considered himself to be a sculptor above all else. He believed his chisels released the sculpture from the stone. This famous sonnet was written in reply to Giovanni Strozzi who said that "the sculpture of the Night for the Medici chapel tomb of Giuliano de' Medici was sculpted by an angel and would speak if awoken":

> *Caro m'è il sonno . . .*
>
> Dear to me is sleep
> in stone while harm and
> shame persist;
> not to see, not to feel, is bliss;
> speak softly, do not wake me,
> do not weep.

1. Part A

What is the author's opinion of Michelangelo's art?

○ A. He thinks that it could have been improved, but was good for the time period.
○ B. He thinks that it is remarkable and has had lasting effects on art.
○ C. He thinks that Michelangelo should have only been a sculptor.
○ D. He thinks that Michelangelo's art is confusing and needs more explanation.

Part B

Which detail from the passage supports your answer to Part A?

○ A. "Michelangelo considered himself to be a sculptor above all else." (paragraph 2)
○ B. "The strength of Michelangelo's work lies in its ability to understand, imitate, and even surpass the classical masters . . ." (paragraph 2)
○ C. "By influencing Italian art he influenced European art . . ." (paragraph 2)
○ D. "He believed his chisels released the sculpture from the stone." (paragraph 2)

2. Part A

What is the meaning of the word **chisels**, as it is used in paragraph 2?

○ A. imagination
○ B. thinking
○ C. tools
○ D. paints

Part B

Which detail from the passage supports your answer to Part A?

○ A. ". . . released the sculpture from the stone." (paragraph 2)
○ B. "This famous sonnet was written in reply . . ." (paragraph 2)
○ C. "Michelangelo considered himself to be a sculptor above all else." (paragraph 2)
○ D. ". . . paintings are monumental milestones . . ." (paragraph 2)

Observe the following pictures closely and read their captions. Then answer the questions that follow.

The *Mona Lisa* was one of Leonardo's favorite paintings, and it remained with him until he died. The smooth, rounded features are similar to some of Leonardo's other portraits of women, and to his paintings of the Virgin Mary. The woman in this portrait has an expression of great dignity and calm. Her mouth hovers at the edge of a smile, giving her a sense of mystery. This is the most celebrated smile in the history of painting.

This detail from *The Creation of Adam* by Michelangelo has been used for various purposes, including advertisements, films, television, and graphics. This is a testament to its fame and everlasting endurance as an icon for more than five hundred years.

3. Select **four** details from the list below that would be supported by either of the artists' paintings.

   ☐ A. "Leonardo gives additional force to his portraits by using plain, dark backgrounds." (paragraph 4)

   ☐ B. "Michelangelo's influence on the course of Western art and architecture has been profound." (paragraph 1)

   ☐ C. "The challenge of drawing the naked human form in complicated poses persists as a test for the would-be artist even today." (paragraph 1)

   ☐ D. "He believed that careful observation led to understanding . . ." (paragraph 2)

   ☐ E. "His use of light and shadow made the figures look solid and lifelike." (paragraph 2)

   ☐ F. "His buildings still dominate Rome today, and his sculptures and paintings are monumental milestones in the course of the history of art." (paragraph 2)

4. You have read two passages about famous artists entitled, ***Leonardo Da Vinci*** and ***Michelangelo and the Renaissance***. You also reviewed a painting by Leonardo da Vinci called the ***Mona Lisa*** and a detail from one of Michelangelo's paintings called ***The Creation of Adam***. Which of the two artists has made more of a contribution to art and society? Be sure to include textual evidence from all three sources to support your answer.

BRAINSTORM HERE

Write your response here:

Answers

Leonardo Da Vinci Passage

1. **Part A: A; Part B: D**   Leonardo painted all of the women as young, beautiful, and serene. He glamorized them in the painting. Therefore, *idealized* means glamorized.

2. **Part A: C; Part B: B**   The passage speaks about Leonardo's observation of how light fell on objects.

3. **Part A: A; Part B: B and C**   The purpose of the passage is to explain how Leonardo Da Vinci became a distinguished painter. It does mention his techniques, his job, and his use of *chiaroscuro*, however, these are details used to show how he developed his talent.

Michelangelo and the Renaissance Passage

1. **Part A: B; Part B: B**   We can tell the author thinks Michelangelo's art is remarkable because he mentions the strength of his art and how it surpasses, or outshines, other masters of art.

2. **Part A: C; Part B: A**   Since chisels release a sculpture from a stone, they are a type of tool which can separate the art from the rest of the rock.

3. **A, B, E, and F**   The *Mona Lisa* illustrates Leonardo da Vinci's use of dark backgrounds, and his use of light and shadow make the painting look lifelike. *The Creation of Adam* detail has been used throughout the centuries and demonstrates how Michelangelo has had influence on Western art and how his paintings are monumental milestones.

4. Read the sample response below. What score do you think it would receive based on the rubric located in Appendix B of this book? Why?

Beautiful, decorative, and monumental are words that come to mind when we think of the Sistine Chapel. It would be hard to find a person who does not know what that is or who painted it. Yet this is only one of the many works of art that Michelangelo created. This is why Michelangelo is the one who has made the biggest contribution to art and our society.

First, Michelangelo was not only a painter, but he was also someone who sculpted. In fact people said that his artwork was "sculpted by an angel . . ." In addition to this sculpture, who hasn't heard of Michelangelo's most famous sculpture, David. This sculpture is still highly respected, many years after Michelangelo created it.

Second, Michelangelo's The Creation of Adam is equally respected and just as well recognized today as it was when he painted it five hundred years ago. This picture has been used for all kinds of purposes from films to television to graphics.

In summary, Michelangelo has made an large contribution to art and society. He was a brilent painter and sculpter. His paintings, especially The Creation of Adam, are still recognized and used 500 years after they were painted, and the buildings he constructed still dominate Rome. Michelangelo had many talents that most people could only dream of having. This is probably why his artwork is still used today.

This would probably receive a score of 2. There should be textual evidence from three sources in this response. This response only has one piece of evidence from one source and another piece of evidence that has no documentation. Also, there is no information to explain the other argument, namely why Leonardo da Vinci did not make more of a contribution than Michelangelo. There are also misspellings and some punctuation mistakes. Let's try this response again. Here is the response one more time, only now improvements have been made.

Beautiful, decorative, and monumental are words that come to mind when we think of the Sistine Chapel. It would be hard to find a person who does not know what that is or who painted it. Yet this is only one of the many works of art that Michelangelo created. This is why Michelangelo is the one who has made the biggest contribution to art and our society.

First, Michelangelo was not only a painter, but a sculptor as well. In fact, his sculptures were so well respected, according to the passage from Michelangelo and the Renaissance by David Spance, Giovanni Strozzi said that, "the sculpture of Night for the Medici chapel tomb of Giuliano de' Medici was sculpted by an angel . . ." In addition to this sculpture, who hasn't heard of Michelangelo's most famous sculpture, David? This sculpture is still highly respected and visible today, many centuries after Michelangelo created it. While Leonardo da Vinci was a wonderful and talented artist, he does not have the recognition of being both a great sculptor and painter as Michelangelo does.

Second, Michelangelo's <u>The Creation of Adam</u> is equally respected and just as well recognized today as it was when he painted it five hundred years ago. According to the detail from <u>The Creation of Adam</u> caption, this picture has been used for all kinds of purposes, from films, to television, to graphics. "This is a testament to its fame and everlasting endurance as an icon . . ." This piece of art is still having an influence over art in the 21st century.

Lastly, Michelangelo was also a talented architect. According to <u>Michelangelo and the Renaissance</u>, "His buildings still dominate Rome today . . ." That comment cannot be made about Leonardo da Vinci, or too many other people, for that matter. Leonardo Da Vinci was skilled at creating portraits. According to the excerpt from <u>Leonardo Da Vinci</u> by Anthony Mason, "He applied what he had learned to his portraits." This shows that Da Vinci is well known for his portraits, unlike Michelangelo who is known for many types of art.

In summary, Michelangelo has made an enormous contribution to art and society. He was a brilliant painter and sculptor. His paintings, especially <u>The Creation of Adam</u>, are still recognized and used 500 years after they were painted, and the buildings he constructed still dominate Rome. Michelangelo had many talents that most people could only dream of having. This is probably why his artwork is still so relevant today.

A Side-by-Side Comparison of the Two Responses	
First Response	**Revised Response**
The writer tells what people thought of Michelangelo.	The writer refers to the source and provides a direct quote.
There are spelling and punctuation mistakes. For example, *brilliant* and *sculptor* are spelled incorrectly and there is a question that does not end with a question mark.	These mistakes are corrected.

A Side-by-Side Comparison of the Two Responses	
First Response	Revised Response
The writer tells facts about Michelangelo.	The writer goes one step further in the second paragraph by mentioning that Leonardo da Vinci did not have the recognition as a sculptor that Michelangelo did. This supports the writer's thesis.
There are four paragraphs to this essay: introduction, one reason and explanation, a second reason without documentation, and a conclusion.	There are five paragraphs to this essay: introduction, three reasons with support and citations, and a conclusion.

Practice Test

Now you will take a sample practice test. Try your best and remember what you have learned in the previous chapters in this book. There will be three sections in this assessment: The Literary Analysis, The Narrative Writing Task, and the Research Simulation Task. All three types of test questions (EBCR, TECR, and PCR) can be found in this assessment. It is a good idea to time yourself to see how long it takes you to complete a section. You can find the answers to this assessment at the end of the chapter. On the actual test, you would most likely see all three types of questions as well. You would be able to write down notes and brainstorm on scrap paper, and then enter your answers on the computer. If you do finish early, remember to review your answers carefully.

IMPORTANT NOTE: Barron's has made every effort to create sample tests that accurately reflect the PARCC Assessment. However, the tests are constantly changing. The following test will still provide a strong framework for sixth-grade students preparing for the assessment. Be sure to consult *www.parcconline.org* for all the latest testing information.

Unit 1 (110 minutes)

Literary Analysis Task

Directions: You will read an excerpt from two novels: *Black Beauty* and *White Fang*. As you read these texts, you will gather information so that you can answer questions and write an essay.

Read the excerpt below from *Black Beauty* by Anna Sewell and answer the questions that follow.

1   Before I was two years old a circumstance happened which I have never forgotten. It was early in the spring; there had been a little frost in the night, and a light mist still hung over the woods and meadows. I and the other

colts were feeding at the lower part of the field when we heard, quite in the distance, what sounded like the cry of dogs. The oldest of the colts raised his head, pricked his ears, and said, "There are the hounds!" and immediately cantered off, followed by the rest of us to the upper part of the field, where we could look over the hedge and see several fields beyond. My mother and an old riding horse of our master's were also standing near, and seemed to know all about it.

2   "They have found a hare," said my mother, "and if they come this way we shall see the hunt."

3   And soon the dogs were all tearing down the field of young wheat next to ours. I never heard such a noise as they made. They did not bark, nor howl, nor whine, but kept on a "yo! yo, o, o! yo! yo, o, o!" at the top of their voices. After them came a number of men on horseback, some of them in green coats, all galloping as fast as they could. The old horse snorted and looked eagerly after them, and we young colts wanted to be galloping with them, but they were soon away into the fields lower down; here it seemed as if they had come to a stand; the dogs left off barking, and ran about every way with their noses to the ground.

4   "They have lost the scent," said the old horse; "perhaps the hare will get off."

5   "What hare?" I said.

6   "Oh! I don't know what hare; likely enough it may be one of our own hares out of the woods; any hare they can find will do for the dogs and men to run after;" and before long the dogs began their "yo! yo, o, o!" again, and back they came altogether at full speed, making straight for our meadow at the part where the high bank and hedge overhang the brook.

7   "Now we shall see the hare," said my mother; and just then a hare wild with fright rushed by and made for the woods. On came the dogs; they burst over the bank, leaped the stream, and came dashing across the field followed by the huntsmen. Six or eight men leaped their horses clean over, close upon the dogs. The hare tried to get through the fence; it was too thick, and she turned sharp round to make for the road, but it was too late; the dogs were upon her with their wild cries; we heard one shriek, and that was the end

of her. One of the huntsmen rode up and whipped off the dogs, who would soon have torn her to pieces. He held her up by the leg torn and bleeding, and all the gentlemen seemed well pleased.

8 As for me, I was so astonished that I did not at first see what was going on by the brook; but when I did look there was a sad sight; two fine horses were down, one was struggling in the stream, and the other was groaning on the grass. One of the riders was getting out of the water covered with mud, the other lay quite still.

9 "His neck is broke," said my mother.

10 "And serve him right, too," said one of the colts.

11 I thought the same, but my mother did not join with us.

12 "Well, no," she said, "you must not say that; but though I am an old horse, and have seen and heard a great deal, I never yet could make out why men are so fond of this sport; they often hurt themselves, often spoil good horses, and tear up the fields, and all for a hare or a fox, or a stag, that they could get more easily some other way; but we are only horses, and don't know."

13 While my mother was saying this we stood and looked on. Many of the riders had gone to the young man; but my master, who had been watching what was going on, was the first to raise him. His head fell back and his arms hung down, and everyone looked very serious. There was no noise now; even the dogs were quiet, and seemed to know that something was wrong. They carried him to our master's house. I heard afterward that it was young George Gordon, the squire's only son, a fine, tall young man, and the pride of his family.

14 There was now riding off in all directions to the doctor's, to the farrier's, and no doubt to Squire Gordon's, to let him know about his son. When Mr. Bond, the farrier, came to look at the black horse that lay groaning on the grass, he felt him all over, and shook his head; one of his legs was broken. Then someone ran to our master's house and came back with a gun; presently there was a loud bang and a dreadful shriek, and then all was still; the black horse moved no more.

15 My mother seemed much troubled; she said she had known that horse for years, and that his name was "Rob Roy"; he was a good horse, and there was no vice in him. She never would go to that part of the field afterward.

16 Not many days after we heard the church-bell tolling for a long time, and looking over the gate we saw a long, strange black coach that was covered with black cloth and was drawn by black horses; after that came another and another and another, and all were black, while the bell kept tolling, tolling. They were carrying young Gordon to the churchyard to bury him. He would never ride again. What they did with Rob Roy I never knew; but 'twas all for one little hare.

1. Part A

How did the tone of the passage change from beginning to end?

- ○ A. At first it was angry, but later it was peaceful.
- ○ B. At first it was happy, but later it was angry.
- ○ C. At first it was energetic, but later it was mournful.
- ○ D. At first it was sad, but later it was energetic.

Part B

Which **two** sentences, when taken together, support your answer to Part A?

- ☐ A. "On came the dogs; they burst over the bank, leaped the stream, and came dashing across the field followed by the huntsmen." (paragraph 7)
- ☐ B. "I thought the same, but my mother did not join with us." (paragraph 11)
- ☐ C. "I and the other colts were feeding at the lower part of the field when we heard, quite in the distance, what sounded like the cry of dogs." (paragraph 1)
- ☐ D. "There was no noise now; even the dogs were quiet, and seemed to know that something was wrong." (paragraph 13)
- ☐ E. "My mother seemed much troubled; she said she had known that horse for years, and that his name was 'Rob Roy'; he was a good horse, and there was no vice in him." (paragraph 15)

2. Part A

What does the word **astonished** mean as it is used in paragraph 8?

○ A. blind
○ B. sad
○ C. happy
○ D. surprised

Part B

Which detail supports your answer to Part A?

○ A. "I thought the same, but my mother did not join with us." (paragraph 11)
○ B. "I did not at first see what was going on by the brook . . ." (paragraph 8)
○ C. "One of the riders was getting out of the water covered with mud . . ." (paragraph 8)
○ D. "'His neck is broke,' said my mother." (paragraph 9)

3. Part A

Which word best describes the mother in the story?

○ A. bitter
○ B. intelligent
○ C. compassionate
○ D. selfish

Part B

Which detail from the story **best** supports your answer to Part A?

○ A. "They have found a hare," said my mother, "and if they come this way we shall see the hunt." (paragraph 2)
○ B. "Oh! I don't know what hare; likely enough it may be one of our own hares out of the woods . . ." (paragraph 6)
○ C. "My mother seemed much troubled; she said she had known that horse for years, and that his name was 'Rob Roy'; he was a good horse . . ." (paragraph 15)
○ D. "'His neck is broke,' said my mother." (paragraph 9)

Now you will read an excerpt from *White Fang*, by Jack London. Answer the questions that follow.

1   He was a fierce little cub. So were his brothers and sisters. It was to be expected. He was a carnivorous animal. He came of a breed of meat-killers and meat-eaters. His father and mother lived wholly upon meat. The milk he had sucked with his first flickering life was milk transformed directly from meat, and now, at a month old, when his eyes had been open for but a week, he was beginning himself to eat meat—meat half-digested by the she-wolf and disgorged for the five growing cubs that already made too great demand upon her breast.

2   But he was, further, the fiercest of the litter. He could make a louder rasping growl than any of them. His tiny rages were much more terrible than theirs. It was he that first learned the trick of rolling a fellow-cub over with a cunning paw-stroke. And it was he that first gripped another cub by the ear and pulled and tugged and growled through jaws tight-clenched. And certainly it was he that caused the mother the most trouble in keeping her litter from the mouth of the cave.

3   The fascination of the light for the grey cub increased from day to day. He was perpetually departing on yard-long adventures toward the cave's entrance, and as perpetually being driven back. Only he did not know it for an entrance. He did not know anything about entrances—passages whereby one goes from one place to another place. He did not know any other place, much less of a way to get there. So to him the entrance of the cave was a wall—a wall of light. As the sun was to the outside dweller, this wall was to him the sun of his world. It attracted him as a candle attracts a moth. He was always striving to attain it. The life that was so swiftly expanding within him, urged him continually toward the wall of light. The life that was within him knew that it was the one way out, the way he was predestined to tread. But he himself did not know anything about it. He did not know there was any outside at all.

4 There was one strange thing about this wall of light. His father (he had already come to recognize his father as the one other dweller in the world, a creature like his mother, who slept near the light and was a bringer of meat)— his father had a way of walking right into the white far wall and disappearing. The grey cub could not understand this. Though never permitted by his mother to approach that wall, he had approached the other walls, and encountered hard obstruction on the end of his tender nose. This hurt. And after several such adventures, he left the walls alone. Without thinking about it, he accepted this disappearing into the wall as a peculiarity of his father, as milk and half-digested meat were peculiarities of his mother.

5 In fact, the grey cub was not given to thinking—at least, to the kind of thinking customary of men. His brain worked in dim ways. Yet his conclusions were as sharp and distinct as those achieved by men. He had a method of accepting things, without questioning the why and wherefore. In reality, this was the act of classification. He was never disturbed over *why* a thing happened. *How* it happened was sufficient for him. Thus, when he had bumped his nose on the back-wall a few times, he accepted that he would not disappear into walls. In the same way he accepted that his father could disappear into walls. But he was not in the least disturbed by desire to find out the reason for the difference between his father and himself. Logic and physics were no part of his mental make-up.

4. Part A

What is the meaning of **perpetually** as it is used in paragraph 3?

- ○ A. never
- ○ B. always
- ○ C. finally
- ○ D. sometimes

Part B

Which part of the sentence from the story supports the answer to Part A?

- ○ A. "He was always striving to attain it." (paragraph 3)
- ○ B. "He did not know anything about entrances . . ." (paragraph 3)
- ○ C. ". . . swiftly expanding with him . . ." (paragraph 3)
- ○ D. ". . . departing on yard-long adventures . . ." (paragraph 3)

5. Part A

What is the tone of the passage?

○ A. cold

○ B. insulting

○ C. amused

○ D. proud

Part B

Which **two** details **best** support your answer to Part A?

☐ A. "He did not know there was any outside at all." (paragraph 3)

☐ B. ". . . he accepted this disappearing into the wall as a peculiarity of his father . . ." (paragraph 4)

☐ C. ". . . he left the walls alone." (paragraph 4)

☐ D. "He could make a louder rasping growl than any of them." (paragraph 2)

☐ E. "It was he that first learned the trick of rolling a fellow-cub over with a cunning paw-stroke." (paragraph 2)

6. Part A

Read this sentence from the passage

> The fascination of the light for the grey cub increased from day to day.

Which statement best describes how this sentence contributes to the development of the plot?

○ A. The sentence demonstrates the cub's awareness of his surroundings that will lead to action.

○ B. The sentence introduces the main conflict of the passage.

○ C. The sentence reflects the cub's knowledge of the unknown.

○ D. The sentence provides the reader with more insight into the cub's environment.

Part B

Which sentence from the passage contributes to the plot in the same way as the sentence in Part A?

☐ A. "He could make a louder rasping growl than any of them." (paragraph 2)

☐ B. "He did not know there was any outside at all." (paragraph 3)

☐ C. "The life that was so swiftly expanding with him, urged him continually toward the wall of light." (paragraph 3)

☐ D. "And it was he that first gripped another cub by the ear and pulled and tugged and growled through jaws tight-clenched." (paragraph 2)

7. You have read excerpts from *Black Beauty* and *White Fang*. Compare and contrast how the authors use points of view to develop the plot of the story. Use details from both stories to support your answer.

BRAINSTORM HERE

Write your response here:

Long Passage Set

Directions: You will be reading a narrative called *Casey at the Bat*. As you read, pay close attention to the characters. You will then be asked to answer questions related to the text.

Read the passage. Then answer the questions.

Casey at the Bat, by Ernest Thayer

1   The outlook wasn't brilliant for the Mudville nine that day;
The score stood four to two, with but one inning more to play,
And then when Cooney died at first, and Barrows did the same,
A pall-like silence fell upon the patrons of the game.

2   A straggling few got up to go in deep despair. The rest
clung to that hope which springs eternal in the human breast;
They thought, "If only Casey could but get a whack at that—
We'd put up even money now, with Casey at the bat."

3   But Flynn preceded Casey, as did also Jimmy Blake,
And the former was a hoodoo, while the latter was a cake;
So upon that stricken multitude grim melancholy sat;
For there seemed but little chance of Casey getting to the bat.

4   But Flynn let drive a single, to the wonderment of all,
And Blake, the much despised, tore the cover off the ball;
And when the dust had lifted, and men saw what had occurred,
There was Jimmy safe at second and Flynn a-hugging third.

5   Then from five thousand throats and more there rose a lusty yell;
It rumbled through the valley, it rattled in the dell;
It pounded on the mountain and recoiled upon the flat,
For Casey, mighty Casey, was advancing to the bat.

6   There was ease in Casey's manner as he stepped into his place;
There was pride in Casey's bearing and a smile lit Casey's face.
And when, responding to the cheers, he lightly doffed his hat,
No stranger in the crowd could doubt 'twas Casey at the bat.

7   Ten thousand eyes were on him as he rubbed his hands with dirt.
Five thousand tongues applauded when he wiped them on his shirt.
Then while the writhing pitcher ground the ball into his hip,
Defiance flashed in Casey's eye, a sneer curled Casey's lip.

8   And now the leather-covered sphere came hurtling through the air,
And Casey stood a-watching it in haughty grandeur there.
Close by the sturdy batsman the ball unheeded sped—
"That ain't my style," said Casey. "Strike one!" the umpire said.

9   From the benches, black with people, there went up a muffled roar,
Like the beating of the storm-waves on a stern and distant shore;
"Kill him! Kill the umpire!" shouted someone on the stand;
And it's likely they'd have killed him had not Casey raised his hand.

10   With a smile of Christian charity great Casey's visage shone;
He stilled the rising tumult; he bade the game go on;
He signaled to the pitcher, and once more the dun sphere flew;
But Casey still ignored it, and the umpire said "Strike two!"

11   "Fraud!" cried the maddened thousands, and echo answered "Fraud!"
But one scornful look from Casey and the audience was awed.
They saw his face grow stern and cold, they saw his muscles strain,
And they knew that Casey wouldn't let that ball go by again.

12   The sneer has fled from Casey's lip, the teeth are clenched in hate;
He pounds with cruel violence his bat upon the plate.
And now the pitcher holds the ball, and now he lets it go,
And now the air is shattered by the force of Casey's blow.

13   Oh, somewhere in this favored land the sun is shining bright,
The band is playing somewhere, and somewhere hearts are light,
And somewhere men are laughing, and little children shout,
But there is no joy in Mudville—mighty Casey has struck out.

Directions: Circle the correct answer for each multiple-choice question. Then answer the open-ended questions on the lines provided.

8. **Part A**

In the stanza 11, the word **awed** most nearly means

- ○ A. intimidated
- ○ B. depressed
- ○ C. yelling
- ○ D. lazy

Part B

Which detail from the narrative **best** supports your answer to Part A?

- ○ A. "But Casey still ignored it . . ." (paragraph 10)
- ○ B. "And they knew that Casey wouldn't let that ball go by again." (paragraph 11)
- ○ C. "But one scornful look from Casey . . ." (paragraph 11)
- ○ D. "'Fraud!' cried the maddened thousands . . ." (paragraph 11)

9. **Part A**

Casey can **best** be described as

- ○ A. quiet
- ○ B. awful
- ○ C. shameful
- ○ D. confident

Part B

Which detail from the story **best** supports your answer to Part A?

- ○ A. "But Casey still ignored it, and the umpire said 'Strike two!'" (paragraph 10)
- ○ B. "There was pride in Casey's bearing and a smile lit Casey's face." (paragraph 6)
- ○ C. "He stilled the rising tumult; he bade the game go on . . ." (paragraph 10)
- ○ D. "And they knew that Casey wouldn't let that ball go by again." (paragraph 11)

10. Part A

Which **best** describes the plot of the passage?

○ A. The home team was winning, their best player comes to bat, and he hits a home run.

○ B. The home team was winning, their best player comes to bat, and he strikes out.

○ C. The home team was losing, their best player comes to bat, and he strikes out.

○ D. The home team was losing, their worst player comes to bat, and he strikes out.

Part B

Which **two** details **best** support your answer to Part A?

☐ A. "But there is no joy in Mudville—mighty Casey has struck out." (paragraph 13)

☐ B. "But Flynn let drive a single, to the wonderment of all . . ." (paragraph 4)

☐ C. "And Blake, the much despised, tore the cover off the ball . . ." (paragraph 4)

☐ D. "There was Jimmy safe at second and Flynn a-hugging third . . ." (paragraph 4)

☐ E. "The outlook wasn't brilliant for the Mudville nine that day . . ." (paragraph 4)

☐ F. "And now the air is shattered by the force of Casey's blow." (paragraph 12)

11. Part A

What can you **infer** about Casey's feelings toward the crowd when they were yelling at the umpire?

○ A. He was proud.

○ B. He was angry.

○ C. He was excited.

○ D. He was surprised.

Part B

Which detail **best** supports your answer to Part A?

○ A. "With a smile of Christian charity great Casey's visage shone . . ." (paragraph 10)

○ B. "He pounds with cruel violence his bat upon the plate." (paragraph 12)

○ C. "They saw his face grow stern and cold, they saw his muscles strain . . ." (paragraph 11)

○ D. "The band is playing somewhere, and somewhere hearts are light . . ." (paragraph 13)

12. Part A

How did the crowd's attitude change from the time Casey came to bat until the end of the story?

- ○ A. At first they were calm, but then they were excited.
- ○ B. At first they were excited, but then they were calm.
- ○ C. At first they were excited, but then they were sorrowful.
- ○ D. At first they were shocked, but then they were excited.

Part B

Which **two** details, when taken together, support your answer to Part A?

- ☐ A. "No stranger in the crowd could doubt 'twas Casey at the bat." (paragraph 6)
- ☐ B. "It rumbled through the valley, it rattled in the dell . . ." (paragraph 5)
- ☐ C. "And when, responding to the cheers, he lightly doffed his hat . . ." (paragraph 6)
- ☐ D. "'Kill him! Kill the umpire!' shouted someone on the stand . . ." (paragraph 9)
- ☐ E. "But there is no joy in Mudville—mighty Casey has struck out." (paragraph 13)

Unit 2 (110 minutes)

Research Simulation Task

Now you will research how people have negatively affected Earth's climate. You will read one excerpt from a book titled *What's the Point of Being Green?* and then you will read a passage from an article titled "Everything but the Carbon Sink." Lastly, you will read an excerpt from a blog entitled "Polar Bears and PCs: Technology's Unintended Consequences." As you review these sources, you will gather information so that you can answer questions and write an essay.

Read the passage taken from *What's the Point of Being Green?* by Jacqui Bailey. Then answer the questions.

(Source A)

What Are We Doing to the Climate?

1   To understand how Earth's climate is changing, it's useful to know a little bit about how it works.

2   Global climate is affected by all sorts of things—the amount of energy (heat and light) coming from the Sun (solar radiation), the atmosphere surrounding Earth, and the ways in which the Sun's energy, the atmosphere, and Earth's surface act together.

It's All in the Atmosphere

3   The only reason we can live on Earth at all is because of its atmosphere. Without it, our planet would be just a dry, lifeless rock spinning in space.

4   The atmosphere is a mixture of gases, dust, and water droplets. These droplets form a barrier around the planet that blocks out most of the Sun's harmful rays but allows some of its heat and light to pass through.

5   The Sun's heat warms the surface of Earth, which then acts like a gigantic radiator by sending heat back into the atmosphere. Some of this surface heat escapes through the atmosphere into space, and some is held within, warming up the air closest to the surface and adding more warmth to the surface itself.

Living in a Greenhouse

6 This process is known as the greenhouse effect because it works like a greenhouse by holding in heat and smoothing out, or lessening, the extremes of hot and cold that happen between day and night.

On the Surface

7 Okay, so we all know that Earth's temperature is entirely smooth and, from our point of view, varies quite a bit from one part of the world to another—otherwise, we could sunbathe at the North Pole or go ice skating on the Amazon.

8 Mainly this is because Earth is round, which means that the Sun's rays shine directly on the equator but are more spread out in the northern and southern parts of the world. It is also because of seasonal changes in Earth's tilt relative to the Sun, because of the winds that carry heat from one place to another, and because of the different ways the land and oceans absorb and release heat.

9 Like winds, oceans also make a big difference by moving heat around. Ocean currents flow around the world carrying hotter and colder water with them and changing the temperature of the air and land nearby.

10 The land varies in the amount of heat it absorbs and releases, depending on what is covering its surface. Large areas of ice, for example, work like mirrors to reflect most of the Sun's heat back into space, keeping the temperatures low in these parts.

Greenhouse Gases

11 The Gases in the atmosphere are mostly nitrogen and oxygen. The rest (about 1 percent) consists of the gas argon, and minuscule amounts of a group of gases known as greenhouse gases (GHGs). These are carbon dioxide, methane, halocarbons, nitrous oxide, and ozone. Together with water vapor, these greenhouse gases are the ONE AND ONLY reason the atmosphere works like a greenhouse.

Global Warming

12 Most of these GHGs exist naturally in the atmosphere and life on Earth would be a lot more difficult without them, but for more than a century we have been adding to them in ways that are unnatural.

13 Scientists now think that by increasing the greenhouse gases in atmosphere, we are strengthening their effect, and it is this that is changing the global climate and making the world warmer.

Leader of the Pack

14 Carbon dioxide (CO_2) is usually seen as the biggest baddy of them all because there is more of it than other GHGs. Carbon dioxide has been in Earth's atmosphere for almost as long as Earth itself, and back in the beginning it was a major part of the atmosphere.

15 Then plants evolved. Plants take in carbon dioxide and use it to make their food, giving out oxygen in the process (it's called photosynthesis). Over millions and millions of years, the plants (especially tiny ocean plants called phytoplankton) removed lots of the carbon dioxide and put oxygen in its place (luckily for us). And because carbon dioxide dissolves in water, some of it is also absorbed by the oceans.

16 But it is not all one way. Carbon dioxide is put back into the atmosphere when plants and animals die and decay, or are burned. It is also produced as a waste product by plants when they use energy to grow, and when animals breathe out.

Changing the Balance

17 Eventually the levels of CO_2 in the atmosphere achieved a balance—until the Industrial Revolution happened and we added motors to machines.

18 Motorized machines radically changed our lives and our world—in many ways for the better (after all, what would we do without the electric toothbrush!). But they also need vast amounts of energy to build them and make them work. Most of that energy comes from burning fossil fuels (coal, oil, and natural gas), and burning fossil fuels produces lots of extra carbon dioxide, known as CO_2 emissions.

To Make Things Worse

19 At the same time, we started clearing away forests (known as deforestation) to make space for more houses, factories, and farm land, chopping down millions of trees that would otherwise help to get rid of all that extra CO_2.

20 On top of that, the trees that are cut down are often burned, which adds more CO_2 to the atmosphere.

21 In fact, burning any vegetation—whether it is trees, grasslands, or leftover crop stubble in fields—contributes to CO_2 emissions.

1. Part A

What is the meaning of **minuscule** as it is used in paragraph 11?

○ A. large
○ B. unimportant
○ C. harmful
○ D. tiny

Part B

Which detail from the story **best** supports your answer to Part A?

○ A. ". . . ONE AND ONLY reason the atmosphere works . . ." (paragraph 11)
○ B. "The rest (about 1 percent) consists of the gas argon . . ." (paragraph 11)
○ C. "Most of these GHGs exist naturally . . ." (paragraph 12)
○ D. ". . . we are strengthening their effect . . ." (paragraph 13)

2. Look at the list of details from the passage. Drag the four most important details, in order, to the boxes below to make a summary of the passage. (In this case, write the details in the boxes.)

(1) "The Sun's heat warms up the surface of Earth, which then acts like a giant radiator by sending heat back into the atmosphere." (paragraph 5)

(2) "Mainly this is because Earth is round, which means that the Sun's rays shine directly on the equator but are more spread out in the northern and southern parts of the world." (paragraph 8)

(3) "Global climate is affected by all sorts of things—the amount of energy (heat and light) coming from the Sun (solar radiation), the atmosphere surrounding Earth, and the ways in which the Sun's energy, the atmosphere, and Earth's surface act together." (paragraph 2)

(4) "Scientists now think that by increasing greenhouse gases in the atmosphere, we are strengthening their effect, and that is changing global climate and making the world warmer." (paragraph 13)

(5) "The rest (about 1 percent) consists of the gas argon, and minuscule amounts of a group of gases known as greenhouse gases." (paragraph 11)

(6) "The land varies in the amount of heat it absorbs and releases, depending on what is covering the surface." (paragraph 10)

3. Part A

What is the author's main purpose for writing this passage?

○ A. to explain Earth's atmosphere to the reader
○ B. to explain how temperatures vary on Earth
○ C. to explain that deforesting is bad
○ D. to explain how people are affecting Earth's climate

Part B

Which detail from the story helps to support your answer to Part A?

○ A. "On top of that the trees that are cut down are often burned . . ."
       (paragraph 20)
○ B. "Most of these GHGs exist naturally in the atmosphere and life on Earth
       would be a lot more difficult without them, but for more than a century we
       have been adding to them in ways that are unnatural." (paragraph 12)
○ C. "The only reason we can live on Earth at all is because of its atmosphere."
       (paragraph 3)
○ D. "Mainly this is because Earth is round, which means that the Sun's rays
       shine directly on the equator but are more spread out in the northern and
       southern parts of the world." (paragraph 8)

You will now read a passage from "Everything but the Carbon Sink," which can be found at *www.naturalinquirer.org*. Answer the questions that follow.

(Source B)

1   Carbon dioxide continually cycles between Earth and the atmosphere. In the past, this cycling created an average balance over time between atmospheric carbon dioxide and carbon on Earth. Over the past 100 years, however, human activities have increased the amount of carbon dioxide released into the atmosphere. Carbon dioxide is released when trees are removed for development and when fossil fuels are burned for energy.

2   Human activities have caused other changes. Tropospheric ozone, another gas, helps protect Earth from the Sun's ultraviolet radiation. When fossil fuels are burned, however, too much ozone is produced near Earth's surface. This ozone contributes to creating a kind of air pollution called smog.

3   Another long-term change involves nitrogen. Human activities have also caused an increase in nitrogen on Earth's surface. Nitrogen is released when fossil fuels are burned for energy. Much of this nitrogen returns to Earth. Nitrogen is also used as a crop fertilizer. Over time or in large amounts, nitrogen adds too much acid to plants, soil, and water bodies. In the short term or in smaller amounts, nitrogen can cause an increase in plant growth. This growth occurs because the plants are able to use nitrogen as a nutrient.

4   The scientists were interested in land use changes over the past 100 years. Over time, for example, forests have been cut and regrown. Farms have been cultivated and abandoned. Land developed for buildings and roads is one type of land use change that is not usually reversed.

4. **Part A**

What is the meaning of **nutrient** as it is used in paragraph 3?

○ A. food
○ B. protection
○ C. barrier
○ D. damage

Part B

Which detail from the story **best** supports your answer to Part A?

○ A. ". . . too much acid to plants, soil, and water bodies." (paragraph 3)
○ B. "This growth occurs because the plants are able to use nitrogen . . ." (paragraph 3)
○ C. "Much of this nitrogen returns to Earth." (paragraph 3)
○ D. "The scientists were interested in land use changes . . ." (paragraph 4)

5. **Part A**

Which of the following is an effect of burning fossil fuels?

○ A. developed land
○ B. forests being cut down
○ C. smog
○ D. ultraviolet radiation

Part B

Which **two** details from the passage, when taken together, support your answer to Part A?

☐ A. "Carbon dioxide continually cycles between Earth and the atmosphere." (paragraph 1)
☐ B. "When fossil fuels are burned, however, too much ozone is produced . . ." (paragraph 2)
☐ C. "Human activities have caused other changes." (paragraph 2)
☐ D. "This ozone contributes to creating a kind of air pollution . . ." (paragraph 2)
☐ E. "Carbon dioxide is released when trees are removed . . ." (paragraph 1)

Now you will read an excerpt from a blog entitled, "Polar Bears and PCs: Technology's Unintended Consequences" (*http://msms.ehe.osu.edu/category/ climate-change/*). Answer the questions that follow.

(Source C)

1   When we talk about the problems of global climate change, we tend to focus on cars and coal-burning power plants as major contributors. Yet there are other significant players, including consumer electronics. The number of cell phones, MP3 players, laptops, and flat-screen TVs is increasing rapidly, and not just in wealthier nations. It is estimated that one in nine people in Africa has a cell phone—and those numbers are expected to continue growing.

2   A recent report from the International Energy Agency (IEA) estimates that new devices such as MP3 players, cell phones, and flat-screen TVs will triple energy consumption. Two hundred new nuclear power plants would be needed just to power all the TVs, iPods, PCs, and other devices expected to be used by 2030.

3   For example, consider televisions. The IEA estimates that 2 billion TVs will soon be in use across the world (an average of 1.3 TVs for every household with electricity). TVs are also getting bigger and being left on for longer periods of time. IEA predicts a 5 percent annual increase in energy consumption between 1990 and 2030 from televisions alone.

4   While consumer electronics is the fastest growing area, it is also the area with the least amount of policies to control energy efficiency. Total greenhouse gas emissions for electronic gadgets is currently at about 500 million tons of carbon dioxide per year. If nothing is done, the IEA estimates that the figure will double to about 1 billion tons of carbon dioxide per year by 2030. However, the agency says that existing technologies could reduce this figure by 30–50 percent at little cost. Allowing consumers to regulate energy consumption based on the features they actually use, minimum-performance standards, and easy-to-read energy labels can help consumers make smarter energy choices about their personal electronics.

6. Part A

In the passage, how does the author indicate that there is something the public can do to reduce the amount of carbon dioxide released into the atmosphere?

- A. The author explains the different types of electronic devices that are consuming energy.
- B. The author states how many televisions will soon be in use in the world.
- C. The author states how many nuclear power plants will be needed to power electronic devices by the year 2030.
- D. The author explains that existing technologies can be used to reduce energy consumption and the amount of carbon dioxide emitted.

Part B

Which detail from the passage supports your answer to Part A?

- A. "For example, consider televisions. The IEA estimates that 2 billion TVs will soon be in use across the world . . ." (paragraph 3)
- B. "Allowing consumers to regulate energy consumption based on the features they actually use, minimum-performance standards, and easy-to-read energy labels can help consumers make smarter energy choices . . ." (paragraph 4)
- C. "Two hundred new nuclear power plants would be needed just to power all the TVs, iPods, PCs, and other devices expected to be used by 2030." (paragraph 2)
- D. "The number of cell phones, MP3 players, laptops, and flat-screen TVs is increasing rapidly, and not just in wealthier nations." (paragraph 1)

7. Select **one** central idea that can be found in all **three** passages. Then select one statement from each text that supports the central idea. (In this case, write the central idea and statements in the correct box.)

Central Idea	What's the Point . . .?	Everything but . . .	Polar Bears . . .
Earth's atmosphere works like a greenhouse.	". . . and burning fossil fuels produces lots of extra carbon dioxide, known as CO_2 emissions."	"Carbon dioxide continually cycles between Earth and the atmosphere."	"Two hundred new nuclear power plants would be needed . . ."
Increased Carbon dioxide emissions are damaging the earth.	"Motorized machines radically changed our lives and our world—in many ways for the better . . ."	"Over the past 100 years, however, human activities have increased the amount of carbon dioxide released into the atmosphere."	"Yet there are other significant players, including consumer electronics."
Motorized equipment has had a negative effect on the environment.	"Carbon dioxide has been in Earth's atmosphere for almost as long as Earth itself . . ."	"Over time, for example, forests have been cut and regrown."	"If nothing is done, the IEA estimates that the figure will double to about 1 billion tons of carbon dioxide per year by 2030."

Central Idea	What's the Point . . .?	Everything but . . .	Polar Bears . . .

8. You have read three passages that claim that people have negatively affected Earth's climate. These passages are: *What's the Point of Being Green?*, "Everything but the Carbon Sink," and "Polar Bears and PCs: Technology's Unintended Consequences." Write an essay that compares and contrasts the evidence each source uses to support this claim. Be sure to include textual evidence from each source to support your answer.

BRAINSTORM HERE

Write your response here:

Short Passage Set

Directions: The following passage is an excerpt from *A Day in the Life of Your Body*, by Beverly McMillan. Read the passage and answer the questions that follow.

Think! Think!

1   When it's test time in school, you rely on the remarkable ability of your brain to process and store information. More than 80 percent of your brain is a region called the cerebrum, which looks like a shelled walnut. Impulses from its billions of nerve cells allow you to think, learn, and remember. The cerebrum also manages abilities such as speaking and writing and sends the orders to muscles when you move some part of your body. Behind and below the cerebrum, the cerebellum helps control movements and balance. The brain stem connects your brain to the spinal cord. It has several important parts that manage the operations of many internal organs, such as your heart and lungs.

Your Thinking Brain

2   Your cerebrum is divided into right and left halves, called hemispheres. The cerebrum's top layer, the cerebral cortex, is the center for the brain's most complex operations, like solving problems. The bodies of cerebral cortex nerve cells form gray matter. Axons form white matter.

Hemispheres in Action

3   The cerebrum's two hemispheres work together on most tasks but, for some "brain work," they divide the labor. In most people, the left hemisphere manages math, language skills, and logical thinking. The right hemisphere handles emotions, and artistic and musical skills. Each hemisphere controls the opposite side of the body. For example, when you move your left leg, the command for this action comes from the right cerebral hemisphere.

Brain Lobes

4   Each half of the cerebrum is divided into regions called lobes. The frontal lobe is concerned with speaking and deliberate movements. The temporal lobe processes hearing and, together with the occipital lobe, it manages vision. The parietal lobe deals with other senses.

Learning, Memory, and Emotions

5   When you learn a fact, remember it, or need to make a decision, your cerebrum's limbic system is active. These parts loop around the brain stem and "talk" constantly with other brain areas. The limbic system is also in charge of emotions.

Why Do Palms Sweat?

6   Hot weather can make you sweat and so can your emotions. The limbic system is the culprit. When you feel nervous or anxious about a school test, your limbic system may send signals that boost the activity of sweat glands.

9. **Part A**

What does the word **culprit** mean as it is used in paragraph 6?

- ○ A. solution
- ○ B. gland
- ○ C. effect
- ○ D. cause

Part B

Which detail from the passage supports your answer to Part A?

- ○ A. "Hot weather can make you sweat . . ." (paragraph 6)
- ○ B. "These parts loop around the brain stem and 'talk' constantly with other brain areas." (paragraph 5)
- ○ C. "When you feel nervous or anxious about a school test, your limbic system may send signals that boost the activity of sweat glands." (paragraph 6)
- ○ D. "When you learn a fact, remember it, or need to make a decision . . ." (paragraph 5)

10. **Part A**

According to the passage, if you throw a ball with your right hand, which hemisphere of the brain would give the command?

- ○ A. right
- ○ B. left
- ○ C. both
- ○ D. neither

Part B

Which detail from the passage supports your answer to Part A?

- ○ A. "Each hemisphere controls the opposite side of the body." (paragraph 3)
- ○ B. "The cerebrum's two hemispheres work together on most tasks." (paragraph 3)
- ○ C. "Your cerebrum is divided into right and left halves, called hemispheres." (paragraph 2)
- ○ D. "The right hemisphere handles emotions, and artistic and musical skills." (paragraph 3)

11. Different parts of the brain are responsible for different functions. Drag each detail to the corresponding part of the brain. There is only one detail for each part. (In this case, just write each detail in the box under the corresponding part of the brain.)

(1) solving problems
(2) writing
(3) connects the brain to the spinal cord
(4) deliberate movements
(5) balance

Cerebrum
Cerebral Cortex
Brain Stem
Cerebellum
Frontal Lobe

12. **Part A**

What is the **main** idea of this passage?

- ○ A. The cerebrum, the largest part of the brain, is in charge of many functions of the body.
- ○ B. The cerebellum controls a person's movement and balance.
- ○ C. The limbic system loops around the brain stem and is in charge of emotions.
- ○ D. The brain stem makes sure that your internal organs are functioning properly.

Part B

Which **two** details, when put together, support your answer to Part A?

- ☐ A. "The limbic system is also in charge of emotions." (paragraph 5)
- ☐ B. "It has several important parts that manage the operations of many internal organs, such as your heart and lungs." (paragraph 1)
- ☐ C. "More than 80 percent of your brain is a region called the cerebrum . . ." (paragraph 1)
- ☐ D. "Behind and below the cerebrum, the cerebellum helps control movements and balance." (paragraph 1)
- ☐ E. "Impulses from its billions of nerve cells allow you to think, learn, and remember." (paragraph 1)

13. **Part A**

Based on the information in the passage, which one of the following may be the effect of a damaged occipital lobe?

- ○ A. A person may have trouble speaking.
- ○ B. A person may have vision loss.
- ○ C. A person may have hearing loss.
- ○ D. A person may have trouble walking.

Part B

Which detail supports your answer to Part A?

- ○ A. "Each half of the cerebrum is divided into regions called lobes." (paragraph 4)
- ○ B. ". . . together with the occipital lobe, it manages vision." (paragraph 4)
- ○ C. "The frontal lobe is concerned with speaking and deliberate movements." (paragraph 4)
- ○ D. ". . . processes hearing . . ." (paragraph 4)

Unit 3 (90 minutes)

Narrative Writing Task

Directions: You will be reading part of a fairy tale entitled, "The Gold Spinner." As you read, pay close attention to the characters. You will then be asked to answer questions to prepare to write a narrative story of your own.

Read the passage. Then answer the questions.

"The Gold Spinner," by Maura McHugh

1   In lands far to the north there resided an industrious woman named Frida whose husband died of an illness early in their marriage, leaving her to fend for herself and her only daughter, Hanna.

2   Frida made her income spinning flax into thread and weaving cloth. As Hanna grew up, Frida taught her how to spin, for it was a family tradition. Yet Hanna showed no aptitude for spinning, or any kind of work. Frida had to nag her to cook, clean, feed the hens, or even light a fire. As Hanna grew into a beautiful girl, Frida worried about how her daughter would make her way in the world if she didn't acquire any skills.

3   One morning after scolding her daughter for her lack of activity, Frida placed a stool on the straw roof of their cottage and ordered her daughter to sit on it and spin. Frida thought it would shame Hanna into work, as she would be in full view of all their neighbors and the travelers on the road.

4   Hanna was a cheerful sort, however, and she used her time on the roof to enjoy the sunshine and see what everyone was up to from her excellent vantage point.

5   That day, Prince Birger rode past with a small retinue of men on their way back from a boar hunt. The sun gleamed on Hanna's hair, attracting the Prince's attention. Intrigued by the strange situation of a pretty girl sitting on top of a cottage, with a distaff and spindle lying idly at her feet, he urged his horse from the road. Frida appeared at her door, attracted by the sound of their arrival, but was flustered by the attention of such noble company.

6 When Prince Birger inquired about Hanna's curious location, Frida answered sarcastically, "She sits there so that everyone can see how clever she is. In fact she's so clever, she can spin gold out of clay and long straw!"

7 Alas, the Prince was an honest, trusting man and failed to notice Frida's exaggerated tone. The kingdom was in dire need of money after an expensive war, and Birger was at a marriageable age. He was struck by Hanna's beauty and believed that marrying her would solve all his problems.

8 Hanna came down from her perch on the roof, and Prince Birger offered to take her with him to the palace to be his consort if she could perform her marvelous feat. Frida turned pale, and realized she would either have to admit she had lied or put her daughter in danger. Before Frida could explain, Hanna agreed to the terms to save her mother from disgrace and punishment.

9 Mother and daughter had only a few moments to say their goodbyes before Hanna was placed on the Prince's mount and they set off for the palace. During the journey the Prince kept up a lively conversation, but Hanna could barely speak because she was so worried. Birger was sincere and kind, but Hanna had no doubts that a girl of her station would not be acceptable to Birger's family without proof of her wondrous talent.

10 Indeed it was the case. King Erik and Queen Matilda were less than pleased when their only son arrived home with a sweet peasant girl, whom he claimed could spin gold out of clay and straw. Birger was easily fooled, as his parents had witnessed before, and they suspected Hanna of trying to trap their son into marriage. "She must spin clay and straw into gold for three nights," King Erik said. "The punishment for defrauding the crown is death."

11 Birger had faith in Hanna, however, and told her so as he left her in a cold, stone tower room with a new distaff and spindle, along with a pail of clay and a bundle of straw.

12 When the door clanged shut, Hanna allowed herself to cry. She looked out of the tower window across the land where her mother's house lay, and wished she was home beside her family hearth. When she turned and saw the spindle and distaff, she burst into fresh tears, for they reminded her of her absent mother and the impossible chore.

13 Suddenly there was an odd grinding noise and an opening appeared in the hall, through which stepped a short, hideous man with a sly smile. Hanna was so taken aback that she stopped crying. He asked why she was in such an agitated state and Hanna told him the truth, for she believed herself doomed.

14 "Don't worry," he told her. "Take these enchanted gloves. If you wear them while spinning, you will create gold from clay and straw." Initially Hanna didn't believe him, but she tried them on and they worked as promised. She knew there must be a price.

15 "I will return for another two nights. If you are able to guess my name, you can keep the gloves and marry the prince, otherwise I will take you home and you'll be my wife."

16 His leer turned her stomach, but Hanna had little choice and agreed to his terms. He chuckled, bowed, and left through the same magical portal by which he had entered.

17 Hanna had labored for many hours by candlelight until she emptied the pail and no straw remained. She fell into an exhausted sleep.

18 The next morning, Prince Birger opened the door, eager to check on her. His eyes shone with delight and pride when he saw the gleaming gold. The King and Queen were called immediately and everyone marveled, although privately the King gave orders to double the guard on Hanna's room that night.

19 Hanna spent the day with Birger, but she was quiet and let him do most of the talking. In her mind, she created long lists of names, desperately trying to guess the identity of the peculiar little man. She became so anxious that she lost her appetite, and after spotting an elderly man begging on the city streets, she put aside some of her food and offered it to him. He blessed her sincerely.

20 That night Hanna was locked back in the tower room with two buckets of clay and two bundles of straw. She put on the gloves and set to work right away. Many hours later, as she was finishing, a grinding sound heralded the short man's arrival. She spent another hour listing all the names she knew. He rocked back and forth on his heels and grinned as he exclaimed, "No!" to all of her suggestions. Eventually Hanna gave up, and the man left after reminding her of the penalty if she didn't name him correctly the following night.

21 Prince Birger and his family were full of praise for Hanna the following morning, and by now the King had enough gold to pay off his debts. Another night would procure him enough money to hold a fabulous wedding for Birger and Hanna. While they showered her with compliments, Hanna said little, and everyone praised her humility and modesty.

22 Unable to eat breakfast, she once again took her food to the street beggar. He noticed her drawn features and red eyes, and asked if there was anything wrong. She outlined the problem, without naming herself as the one in trouble. The man watched her carefully as she recounted her story, and told her she should have a heart for her "friend."

23 Hanna quickly returned to the palace and raided its library, seeking unusual exotic names. Later that afternoon, Prince Birger sought her out and, seeing her listless and somber mood, tried to cheer her up.

24 "My darling," he said—for he was truly in love with her now—"let me relate an odd story that happened today. On our way home from the hunt this morning, an old man in the street directed us to a new place to find game. Since it was an area I'd never tried before, I decided we should try our luck."

25 "It was a longer ride than usual, up a small mountain. During the hunt I became separated from my men. As I searched for them I spied smoke from a fire and followed it. Through the bushes I saw the strangest little man capering around the fire outside a cave entrance singing this song:

'Tomorrow a fair beauty I will marry,

For few can find my hidden eyrie,

And no one outside of faerie,

Knows my name is Titteli Ture.'

"At that point I heard the hunter's horn and I followed it back to my companions."

26 Upon hearing the story, Hanna sat bolt upright, her eyes brimming with hope. That night, the King left her with three buckets of clay and three bundles of straw. Hanna attacked the job with a happy spirit. At one point she laughed when she considered how surprised her mother would be if she could see her daughter working so hard. By the time she had finished, a rosy dawn painted the sky. Then came the familiar grinding noise and the man danced out of his portal, grinning from ear to ear.

27 Hanna restrained her urge to smile and suggested new names. At last impatient, he said, "One final guess, my love, before we depart for our wedding."

28 She tapped her chin as if in deep thought, then said, "Is it …Titteli Ture?"

1. Part A

How does Hanna's attitude change during the fairy tale?

- ○ A. At first she is shy, but then she becomes outgoing.
- ○ B. At first she is lazy, but then she becomes hardworking.
- ○ C. At first she is friendly, but then becomes mean.
- ○ D. At first she is funny, but then becomes serious.

Part B

Which **two** sentences, when taken together, **best** support your answer to Part A?

- ☐ A. "Unable to eat breakfast, she once again took her food to the street beggar." (paragraph 22)
- ☐ B. "That night, Hanna was locked back in the tower room with two buckets of clay and two bundles of straw." (paragraph 20)
- ☐ C. "Yet Hanna showed no aptitude for spinning, or any kind of work." (paragraph 2)
- ☐ D. "Hanna was a cheerful sort, however, and used her time on the roof to enjoy the sunshine and see what everyone was up to from her excellent vantage point." (paragraph 4)
- ☐ E. "At one point she laughed when she considered how surprised her mother would be if she could see her working so hard." (paragraph 26)
- ☐ F. "Upon hearing the story, Hanna sat bolt upright, her eyes brimming with hope." (paragraph 26)

2. Part A

How does paragraph 12 contribute to the setting of the fairy tale?

○ A. It establishes a funny, light-hearted setting.
○ B. It establishes a critical, dangerous setting.
○ C. It establishes a gloomy, depressing setting.
○ D. It establishes an outrageous, irrational setting.

Part B

Which other paragraph best contributes to the setting in the same way as the answer to Part A?

○ A. Paragraph 9
○ B. Paragraph 17
○ C. Paragraph 7
○ D. Paragraph 26

3. Part A

Which of the following statements **best** states the theme of the fairy tale?

○ A. Hard work and kindness pay off in the end.
○ B. Crime does not pay.
○ C. Love conquers all.
○ D. Family is more important than anything.

Part B

Which detail **best** supports your answer to Part A?

○ A. "Prince Birger and his family were full of praise for Hanna the following morning, and by now the King had enough gold to pay off his debts." (paragraph 21)
○ B. "Hanna spent the day with Birger, but she was quiet and let him do most of the talking." (paragraph 19)
○ C. "Hanna labored for many hours by candlelight until she emptied the pail and no straw remained." (paragraph 17)
○ D. "Alas, the prince was an honest, trusting man and failed to notice Frida's exaggerated tone." (paragraph 7)

4. Part A

What does the word **inquired** mean as used in paragraph 6?

- ○ A. discussed
- ○ B. thought
- ○ C. asked
- ○ D. wondered

Part B

Which detail from the fairy tale best supports the answer to Part A?

- ○ A. "... she can spin gold out of clay ..." (paragraph 6)
- ○ B. "... Frida's exaggerated tone." (paragraph 7)
- ○ C. "... was struck by Hanna's beauty ..." (paragraph 7)
- ○ D. "... Frida answered sarcastically ..." (paragraph 6)

5. In the passage from "The Gold Spinner," the author creates the character, Titteli Ture. Think about the details the author uses to establish his role in the fairy tale.

Directions: Write an original story about what happens after Titteli Ture hears Hanna speak his name. In your story, be sure to use what you have learned about the character as you tell what happens next.

BRAINSTORM HERE

Write your response here:

Paired Passage Set

You will be reading two fictional stories about animals. The first is "Iktomi and the Muskrat." The second is "Granny Shows Reddy a Trick." Think carefully about what you read. You will then answer questions about each story, as well as one question about both.

Read the Dakota legend "Iktomi and the Muskrat," by Zitkala-Sa. Answer the questions that follow.

1   Beside a white lake, beneath a large grown willow tree, sat Iktomi on the bare ground. The heap of smoldering ashes told of a recent open fire. With ankles crossed together around a pot of soup, Iktomi bent over some delicious boiled fish.

2   Fast he dipped his black horn spoon into the soup, for he was ravenous. Iktomi had no regular meal times. Often when he was hungry he went without food.

3   Well hid between the lake and the wild rice, he looked nowhere save into the pot of fish. Not knowing when the next meal would be, he meant to eat enough now to last some time.

4   "How, how, my friend!" said a voice out of the wild rice. Iktomi started. He almost choked with his soup. He peered through the long reeds from where he sat with his long horn spoon in mid-air.

5   "How, my friend!" said the voice again, this time close at his side. Iktomi turned and there stood a dripping muskrat who had just come out of the lake.

6   "Oh, it is my friend who startled me. I wondered if among the wild rice some spirit voice was talking. How, how, my friend!" said Iktomi. The muskrat stood smiling. On his lips hung a ready "Yes, my friend," when Iktomi would ask, "My friend, will you sit down beside me and share my food?"

7   That was the custom of the plains people. Yet Iktomi sat silent. He hummed an old dance-song and beat gently on the edge of the pot with his buffalo-horn spoon. The muskrat began to feel awkward before such lack of hospitality and wished himself under water.

8   After many heart throbs Iktomi stopped drumming with his horn ladle, and looking upward into the muskrat's face, he said:

9   "My friend, let us run a race to see who shall win this pot of fish. If I win, I shall not need to share it with you. If you win, you shall have half of it." Springing to his feet, Iktomi began at once to tighten the belt about his waist.

10   "My friend Ikto, I cannot run a race with you! I am not a swift runner, and you are nimble as a deer. We shall not run any race together," answered the hungry muskrat.

11   For a moment Iktomi stood with a hand on his long protruding chin. His eyes were fixed upon something in the air. The muskrat looked out of the corners of his eyes without moving his head. He watched the wily Iktomi concocting a plot.

12   "Yes, yes," said Iktomi, suddenly turning his gaze upon the unwelcome visitor;

13   "I shall carry a large stone on my back. That will slacken my usual speed; and the race will be a fair one."

14   Saying this he laid a firm hand upon the muskrat's shoulder and started off along the edge of the lake. When they reached the opposite side Iktomi pried about in search of a heavy stone.

15   He found one half-buried in the shallow water. Pulling it out upon dry land, he wrapped it in his blanket.

16   "Now, my friend, you shall run on the left side of the lake, I on the other. The race is for the boiled fish in yonder kettle!" said Iktomi.

17   The muskrat helped to lift the heavy stone upon Iktomi's back. Then they parted. Each took a narrow path through the tall reeds fringing the shore. Iktomi found his load a heavy one. Perspiration hung like beads on his brow. His chest heaved hard and fast.

18   He looked across the lake to see how far the muskrat had gone, but nowhere did he see any sign of him. "Well, he is running low under the wild rice!" said he. Yet as he scanned the tall grasses on the lake shore, he saw not one stir as if to make way for the runner. "Ah, has he gone so fast ahead that the disturbed grasses in his trail have quieted again?" exclaimed Iktomi. With that thought he quickly dropped the heavy stone. "No more of this!" said he, patting his chest with both hands.

19 Off with a springing bound, he ran swiftly toward the goal. Tufts of reeds and grass fell flat under his feet. Hardly had they raised their heads when Iktomi was many paces gone.

20 Soon he reached the heap of cold ashes. Iktomi halted stiff as if he had struck an invisible cliff. His black eyes showed a ring of white about them as he stared at the empty ground. There was no pot of boiled fish! There was no water-man in sight! "Oh, if only I had shared my food like a real Dakota, I would not have lost it all! Why did I not know the muskrat would run through the water? He swims faster than I could ever run! That is what he has done. He has laughed at me for carrying a weight on my back while he shot hither like an arrow!"

21 Crying thus to himself, Iktomi stepped to the water's brink. He stooped forward with a hand on each bent knee and peeped far into the deep water.

22 "There!" he exclaimed, "I see you, my friend, sitting with your ankles wound around my little pot of fish! My friend, I am hungry. Give me a bone!"

23 "Ha! ha! ha!" laughed the water-man, the muskrat. The sound did not rise up out of the lake, for it came down from overhead. With his hands still on his knees, Iktomi turned his face upward into the great willow tree. Opening wide his mouth he begged, "My friend, my friend, give me a bone to gnaw!"

24 "Ha! ha!" laughed the muskrat, and leaning over the limb he sat upon, he let fall a small sharp bone which dropped right into Iktomi's throat. Iktomi almost choked to death before he could get it out. In the tree the muskrat sat laughing loud. "Next time, say to a visiting friend, 'Be seated beside me, my friend. Let me share with you my food.'"

6. Part A

In paragraph 1, the word **smoldering** is used to mean

○ A. glowing
○ B. warming
○ C. black
○ D. burning

Part B

Which detail from the passage **best** supports your answer to Part A?

○ A. ". . . told of a recent open fire." (paragraph 1)
○ B. "With ankles crossed together around a pot of soup . . ." (paragraph 1)
○ C. "Often when he was hungry he went without food." (paragraph 2)
○ D. "Iktomi had no regular meal times." (paragraph 2)

7. Part A

Iktomi can **best** be described as

○ A. generous
○ B. clever
○ C. quiet
○ D. selfish

Part B

Drag the two details that, when read together, **best** support your answer to Part A, to the box. (In this case, just write the two details.)

(1) "Yet Iktomi sat silent." (paragraph 7)
(2) "…when Iktomi was many paces gone." (paragraph 19)
(3) "That was the custom of the plains people." (paragraph 7)
(4) "…Iktomi pried about in search of a heavy stone." (paragraph 14)

8. Part A

The muskrat in the story can best be described as

- ○ A. clever
- ○ B. hungry
- ○ C. selfish
- ○ D. mean

Part B

Which sentence **best** supports your answer to Part A?

- ○ A. "That will slacken my usual speed; and the race will be a fair one." (paragraph 13)
- ○ B. "The muskrat stood smiling." (paragraph 6)
- ○ C. "The muskrat looked out of the corners of his eyes without moving his head." (paragraph 11)
- ○ D. "Why did I not know the muskrat would run through the water?" (paragraph 20)

Now read the following passage from "Granny Shows Reddy a Trick," by Thorton W. Burgess, and answer the questions that follow.

1 Every day Granny Fox led Reddy Fox over to the long railroad bridge and made him run back and forth across it until he had no fear of it whatever. At first it had made him dizzy, but now he could run across at the top of his speed and not mind it in the least. "I don't see what good it does to be able to run across a bridge; anyone can do that!" exclaimed Reddy one day.

2 Granny Fox smiled. "Do you remember the first time you tried to do it?" she asked.

3 Reddy hung his head. Of course he remembered—remembered that Granny had had to scare him into crossing that first time.

4 Suddenly Granny Fox lifted her head. "Hark!" she exclaimed.

5 Reddy pricked up his sharp, pointed ears. Way off back, in the direction from which they had come, they heard the baying of a dog. It wasn't the voice of Bowser the Hound but of a younger dog. Granny listened for a few minutes. The voice of the dog grew louder as it drew nearer.

6 "He certainly is following our track," said Granny Fox. "Now, Reddy, you run across the bridge and watch from the top of the little hill over there. Perhaps I can show you a trick that will teach you why I have made you learn to run across the bridge."

7 Reddy trotted across the long bridge and up to the top of the hill, as Granny had told him to. Then he sat down to watch. Granny trotted out in the middle of a field and sat down. Pretty soon a young hound broke out of the bushes, his nose in Granny's track. Then he looked up and saw her, and his voice grew still more savage and eager. Granny Fox started to run as soon as she was sure that the hound had seen her, but she did not run very fast. Reddy did not know what to make of it, for Granny seemed simply to be playing with the hound and not really trying to get away from him at all.

8 Pretty soon Reddy heard another sound. It was a long, low rumble. Then there was a distant whistle. It was a train.

9 Granny heard it, too. As she ran, she began to work back toward the long bridge. The train was in sight now. Suddenly Granny Fox started across the bridge so fast that she looked like a little red streak. The dog was close at her heels when she started and he was so eager to catch her that he didn't see either the bridge or the train. But he couldn't begin to run as fast as Granny Fox. Oh, my, no! When she had reached the other side, he wasn't halfway across, and right behind him, whistling for him to get out of the way, was the train.

10 The hound gave one frightened yelp, and then he did the only thing he could do; he leaped down, down into the swift water below, and the last Reddy saw of him he was frantically trying to swim ashore.

11 "Now you know why I wanted you to learn to cross a bridge; it's a very nice way of getting rid of dogs," said Granny Fox, as she climbed up beside Reddy.

9. Part A

One of the themes of "Granny Shows Reddy a Trick" can be

- ○ A. good versus evil
- ○ B. will to survive
- ○ C. wisdom of experience
- ○ D. youth and beauty

Part B

Which detail from the passage **best** supports your answer to Part A?

- ○ A. "Now you know why I wanted you to learn to cross a bridge; it's a very nice way of getting rid of dogs . . ." (paragraph 11)
- ○ B. "Granny listened for a few minutes." (paragraph 5)
- ○ C. "'He certainly is following our track,' said Granny Fox." (paragraph 6)
- ○ D. "Reddy did not know what to make of it, for Granny seemed simply to be playing with the hound and not really trying to get away from him at all." (paragraph 7)

10. Identify **five** details from the list that should be included in a summary of the passage. Drag five of the following details to the boxes in **chronological** order. (In this case, write the details in the box in chronological order.)

(1) "'Now you know why I wanted you to learn to cross a bridge; it's a very nice way of getting rid of dogs,' said Granny Fox, as she climbed up beside Reddy." (paragraph 11)

(2) "When she had reached the other side, he wasn't halfway across, and right behind him, whistling for him to get out of the way, was the train." (paragraph 9)

(3) "Of course he remembered—remembered that Granny had had to scare him into crossing that first time." (paragraph 3)

(4) "Perhaps I can show you a trick that will teach you why I have made you learn to run across the bridge." (paragraph 6)

(5) "Suddenly Granny Fox started across the bridge so fast that she looked like a little red streak." (paragraph 9)

(6) "Pretty soon a young hound broke out of the bushes, his nose in Granny's track." (paragraph 7)

(7) "Reddy did not know what to make of it, for Granny seemed simply to be playing with the hound and not really trying to get away from him at all." (paragraph 7)

<table>
<tr><td>

</td></tr>
<tr><td>
</td></tr>
<tr><td>

</td></tr>
<tr><td>

</td></tr>
<tr><td>
</td></tr>
</table>

11. Read the list of central ideas and decide if each one can be found in "**Iktomi and the Muskrat**," "**Granny Shows Reddy a Trick**," or both. Drag each idea to the proper box. (In this case, just write each idea in the correct box.)

It is always good to share.

Sometimes you have to listen to those with more experience.

Watch and learn.

Things are not always as they seem.

"Iktomi and the Muskrat"	Both	"Granny Shows Reddy a Trick"

STOP

This is the end of the test.
Review your answers.

Answers

Unit 1

Literary Analysis Task

Passage	Question	Answer(s)	Explanation
Black Beauty	1A 1B	C A, D	Initially, there is a lot of energy while the hunt is on. However, after the accident, the animals realize that there are severe injuries and the tone changes to mournful.
	2A 2B	D B	The main character is so astonished, or surprised, by what happened that he didn't even notice what was going on by the brook.
	3A 3B	C C	The mother is compassionate. We see this in her being upset over the horse being hurt. We also see it when she is upset when the man is killed.
White Fang	4A 4B	B A	The cub was perpetually striving to get to the entrance of the cave. He always did this, therefore perpetually means always.
	5A 5B	D D, E	The tone is proud, as the author mentions the many ways in which the cub was the best of the group.
	6A	A	The cub was fascinated with the light. This light made him want to discover more about it. This curiosity encouraged the cub to take action.
	6B	C	This sentence tells the reader that the cub was drawn to the wall of light. It contributes to the plot in the same way as the original sentence in that it indicates the cub's awareness of his surroundings.

Passage	Question	Answer(s)	Explanation
Black Beauty/ White Fang	7	**Essay**	This response would probably receive a score of 3.

Literary Analysis Task Sample Response

Black Beauty by Anna Sewell and White Fang by Jack London are about animals reacting to their environment. In Black Beauty, animals are reacting to a hare hunt. In White Fang, the cub is reacting to his family and life in the cave. Both authors use different points of view to develop the plot of the story. Anna Sewell uses first-person point of view, where one of the horses is telling the story. Jack London uses third-person point of view, where a narrator tells what is happening in the story. Through these different points of view, the reader can learn about what is happening in each story.

In Black Beauty, the horse tells about a time when he was a colt and witnessed a hare hunt. During the hunt a hunter was thrown from the horse and was killed. The horse was also hurt and then killed. The reader learns all of this through the colt's perspective and feelings. In paragraph 14 it states, "Then someone ran to our master's house and came back with a gun; presently there was a loud bang and a dreadful shriek, and then all was still; the black horse moved no more" (Sewell). This shows what the colt saw and heard and what he thought of it. It was dreadful. This lets the reader know what is happening and how the characters feel about it.

In White Fang, the narrator tells about the cub and his experience with the cave. In paragraph 4 it states, "The grey cub could not understand this. Though never permitted by his mother to approach that wall, he had approached the other walls, and had encountered hard obstruction on the end of his tender nose" (London). This shows what the cub was doing and how he really didn't understand his environment. However, because it is third-person point of view, the reader does not know the cub's thoughts, as in Black Beauty.

In conclusion, the authors of both stories, Black Beauty and White Fang, develop the plot through different points of view. Black Beauty is written in first person, where the horse tells the reader about the hunt and how he feels when the other horse is killed. White Fang is written in third person, where the narrator tells what is happening in the story, but cannot tell the thoughts of the cub. Both stories have a plot where the main characters are animals reacting to what is happening to them.

Long Passage Set

Passage	Question	Answer(s)	Explanation
Casey at the Bat	8A	A	Casey gave the crowd a scornful, or critical, look and the crowd felt intimidated by it.
	8B	C	
	9A	D	Casey was full of pride and confidence that he would hit the ball when he came to bat.
	9B	B	
	10A	C	The team was losing. Then Casey, their best player, came to bat. In the end, he struck out.
	10B	A, E	
	11A	B	Casey's face grew stern, or very serious, and cold because he was angry at how the people were acting.
	11B	C	
	12A	C	At first, the crowd was very excited to see Casey at bat. Unfortunately, after he struck out, they were sorrowful because their team lost the game.
	12B	C, E	

Unit 2

Research Simulation Task

Passage	Question	Answer(s)	Explanation
What's the Point of Being Green?	1A 1B	D B	Only about 1% of Earth's atmosphere is made up of argon and GHGs. So less than 1% is minuscule, or tiny, compared with the rest of the atmosphere.
	2A	3, 1, 5, 4	These are the most important details that make up the main idea of the passage in chronological order.
	3A 3B	D B	The author's purpose for this passage is to explain how people are affecting Earth's climate. The other details may be part of the passage, but only support the main idea.
"Everything but the Carbon Sink"	4A 4B	A B	Nitrogen is a nutrient that helps plants to grow just as food helps humans to grow. Therefore, nitrogen is food for plants.
	5A 5B	C D	When fossil fuels are produced, so is ozone. Too much ozone creates smog.
"Polar Bears and PCs"	6A 6B	D B	Allowing consumers (people) to control energy consumption is one way to reduce carbon dioxide.
All 3 Texts	7	See chart on next page	
All 3 Texts	8	Essay	This response would probably receive a score of 4.

Central Idea	What's the Point of Being Green?	"Everything but the Carbon Sink"	"Polar Bears and PCs"
Increased carbon dioxide emissions are damaging the earth.	". . . and burning fossil fuels produces lots of extra carbon dioxide, known as CO_2 emissions."	"Over the past 100 years, however, human activities have increased the amount of carbon dioxide released into the atmosphere."	"If nothing is done, the IEA estimates that the figure will double to about 1 billion tons of carbon dioxide per year by 2030."

Research Simulation Sample Response

Who would have thought that the substance we breathe out could actually be damaging Earth's atmosphere? Carbon dioxide is an invisible gas that is causing some pretty visible problems for our environment. The three sources: What's the Point of Being Green? by Jacqui Bailey, "Everything but the Carbon Sink" from www.naturalinquirer.org, and "Polar Bears and PCs: Technology's Unintended Consequences" blog provide evidence that people are contributing extra, harmful carbon dioxide into the environment.

What's the Point of Being Green? discusses the unnatural ways people are contributing carbon dioxide to the environment. Using motorized machines and burning fossil fuels causes too much carbon dioxide to be released in the environment. This is one of the greenhouse gases. In paragraph 13 it states, "Scientists now think that by increasing greenhouse gases in atmosphere, we are strengthening their effect, and it is this that is changing the global climate and making the world warmer" (Bailey). This shows that by people producing too much carbon dioxide, the climate is changing.

In "Everything but the Carbon Sink," the author also talks about people contributing to the carbon dioxide in the atmosphere by burning fossil fuels. However, this article also talks about the fact that burning fossil fuels can also cause smog. In paragraph 2 it states, "When fossil fuels are burned, however, too much ozone is produced near Earth's surface. This ozone contributes to creating a kind of air pollution called smog." This shows that burning fossil fuels contributes to air pollution in addition to affecting Earth's climate.

"Polar Bears and PCs: Technology's Unintended Consequences" does state that cars and fossil fuel coal-burning power plants are major contributors to global climate change. However, it also states how consumer electronics contribute to the release of carbon dioxide in the atmosphere. In paragraph 4 it states, "Total greenhouse gas emissions for electronic gadgets is currently at about 500 million tons of carbon dioxide per year." This shows how much carbon dioxide is released in the atmosphere by people using electronics such as iPods and TVs.

In conclusion, What's the Point of Being Green?, "Everything but the Carbon Sink," and "Polar Bears and PCs: Technology's Unintended Consequences" all discuss how people are causing too much carbon dioxide to be released in the environment. People release carbon dioxide by burning fossil fuels, using motorized equipment, and electronics. These actions affect the Earth's climate and create smog. People should think about how their daily activities affect our planet before it is too late.

Passage	Question	Answer(s)	Explanation
A Day in the Life of Your Body	9A	D	The limbic system is the culprit because it causes your sweat glands to be active.
	9B	C	
	10A	B	Each hemisphere controls the other side of the body. Therefore, the left part of your brain is controlling your right hand.
	10B	A	
	11	Cerebrum: writing Cerebral Cortex: solving problems Brain Stem: connects the brain to the spinal cord Cerebellum: balance Frontal Lobe: deliberate movements	
	12A	A	This passage is mainly about the cerebrum and its functions.
	12B	C, E	
	13A	B	The parietal and occipital lobes manage vision. If either is damaged, a person may have vision loss.
	13B	B	

Unit 3

Narrative Writing Task

Passage	Question	Answer(s)	Explanation
"The Gold Spinner"	1A 1B	B C, E	At first Hanna was always trying to avoid doing work. However, by the end of the passage, she had to work hard to spin the clay and straw into gold so she could marry the Prince.
	2A 2B	C A	Both paragraphs describe situations in which Hanna is in a gloomy or depressing setting.
	3A 3B	A C	Once Hanna worked hard and shared what she had, she was finally able to earn the trust of the King and Queen and figure out the name of the man.
	4A 4B	C D	The Prince inquired, or asked about Hanna. Her mother answered his question sarcastically.
	5	Essay	This essay would probably receive a score of 4.

Narrative Writing Task Sample Response

"What did you say!" shrieked Titteli Ture.

"Tit-tel-i Tu-re," Hanna replied slowly, to make sure that the little man knew she had beat him at his own game.

"This is impossible! How could you..."

"It does not matter how I have come to know your name. It just matters that I do know it." Hanna interrupted.

Immediately, Hanna heard the grinding noise and the opening appeared once again. Titteli Ture grabbed Hanna and dragged her into the hole with him. They were whisked to the center of town and passed the old beggar. Hanna tried to call out to the beggar, but Titteli Ture covered her mouth with his grimy, hairy hands.

At that moment, the Prince came in to check on Hanna. Seeing the room empty, he called out to his parents.

"Hanna is gone! Hanna is gone! What has happened to her?" he inquired with a desperate sound in his voice.

"Get the horses, we must find her at once!" was all the King could manage to say, as he was shocked that Hanna had seemed to disappear.

As they reached the center of town, once again the old beggar spoke to the Prince. "Go back to the place where you hunted game. That is where you will find your love."

Prince Birger found the cave opening once again. Through the trees he could see Titteli Ture. Next to him was his beloved Hanna, tied to a tree by a rope. Titteli Ture was singing once again:

Today I will marry Hanna my love.

She can spin straw into gold because of my glove.

She is so beautiful, she is so pure.

If she isn't, my name is not Titteli Ture.

Instantly Birger leapt in with his horse, knocked Titteli Ture to the ground unconscious, and cut the rope with his sword to release Hanna.

"I'm sorry I deceived you," Hanna said with her head hanging low. "I just tried to save my mother."

"It doesn't matter," Birger replied, "I love you. All the gold . . . all the debts . . . you saved us Hanna." With that he got on one knee. "Marry me?"

"Of course I will!" exclaimed Hanna with delight.

The King and Queen congratulated the couple and offered to throw them the biggest wedding the kingdom had ever seen. All of the kingdom was invited, including the old beggar. He had a seat at the royal table. He even had a new suit to wear, made by Hanna herself. She had finally learned the importance of hard work and never took anything for granted again.

Long Passage Set

Passage	Question	Answer(s)	Explanation
"Iktomi and the Muskrat"	6A	D	The heap of ashes was still burning from the recent fire.
	6B	A	
	7A	D	The custom of the people was to offer and share food. Instead, Iktomi sat silent because he was too selfish to share.
	7B	1, 3	
	8A	A	The muskrat was clever enough to use his ability to quickly swim to win the race.
	8B	D	
"Granny Shows Reddy a Trick"	9A	C	Reddy didn't understand what Granny was trying to teach him at first. She had enough experience to know the best way to get rid of a dog.
	9B	A	
	10	6, 7, 5, 2, 1	These are the most important details in chronological order.
"Iktomi and the Muskrat" "Granny Shows Reddy a Trick"	11	Iktomi—It's always good to share. Granny—(1) Sometimes you have to listen to those with more experience. (2) Watch and learn. Both—Things are not always as they seem.	

Point Scoring Rubric for Narrative Writing Task

Narrative Task

Construct Measured	
Writing and Expression	
Score Point 4	The student response is **effectively** developed with narrative elements and is **consistently appropriate** to the task; demonstrates **purposeful** coherence, clarity, and cohesion, making it **easy to follow** the writer's progression of ideas; establishes and maintains an **effective** style, attending to the norms and conventions of the discipline.
Score Point 3	The student response is **mostly effectively** developed with narrative elements and is **mostly appropriate** to the task; demonstrates coherence, clarity, and cohesion, making it **fairly easy to follow** the writer's progression of ideas; establishes and maintains a **mostly effective** style, while attending to the norms and conventions of the discipline.
Score Point 2	The student response is developed with **some** narrative elements and is **somewhat appropriate** to the task; demonstrates **some** coherence, clarity, and/or cohesion, making the writer's progression of ideas **usually discernible but not obvious**; has a style that is **somewhat** effective, **generally** attending to the norms and conventions of the discipline.
Score Point 1	The student response is **minimally** developed with **few** narrative elements and is **limited in its appropriateness** to the task; demonstrates **limited** coherence, clarity, and/or cohesion, making the writer's progression of ideas **somewhat unclear**; has a style that has **limited** effectiveness, with **limited** awareness of the norms of the discipline.
Score Point 0	The student response is **undeveloped** and/or **inappropriate** to the task; **lacks** coherence, clarity, and cohesion; has an **inappropriate** style, with **little to no** awareness of the norms of the discipline.

Construct Measured	
Writing Knowledge of Language and Conventions	
Score Point 3	The student response to the prompt demonstrates **full command** of the conventions of standard English at an appropriate level of complexity. There may be a **few minor errors** in mechanics, grammar, and usage, but **meaning is clear.**
Score Point 2	The student response to the prompt demonstrates **some command** of the conventions of standard English at an appropriate level of complexity. There **may be errors** in mechanics, grammar, and usage that **occasionally impede understanding**, but the **meaning is generally clear.**
Score Point 1	The student response to the prompt demonstrates **limited command** of the conventions of standard English at an appropriate level of complexity. There **may be errors** in mechanics, grammar, and usage that **often impede understanding.**
Score Point 0	The student response to the prompt demonstrates **no command** of the conventions of standard English. **Frequent and varied errors** in mechanics, grammar, and usage **impede understanding.**

*This rubric is subject to further refinement based on research and study.
For updates, go to http://www.parcconline.org.news

Point Scoring Rubric for Research Simulation Task and Literary Analysis Task

Research Simulation and Literary Task

Construct Measured	
Reading Comprehension for Key Ideas and Details	
Score Point 4	The student response demonstrates **full comprehension** of ideas stated explicitly and inferentially by providing an **accurate** analysis and supporting the analysis with **effective and convincing** textual evidence.
Score Point 3	The student response demonstrates **comprehension** of ideas stated explicitly and/or inferentially by providing a **mostly accurate** analysis and supporting the analysis with **adequate** textual evidence.
Score Point 2	The student response demonstrates **basic comprehension** of ideas stated explicitly and/or inferentially by providing a **generally accurate** analysis and supporting the analysis with **basic** textual evidence.
Score Point 1	The student response demonstrates **limited comprehension** of ideas stated explicitly and/or inferentially by providing a **minimally accurate** analysis and supporting the analysis with **limited** textual evidence.
Score Point 0	The student response demonstrates **no comprehension** of ideas by providing inaccurate or no analysis and **little to no** textual evidence.

Construct Measured	
Writing and Written Expression	
Score Point 4	The student response addresses the prompt and provides **effective and comprehensive** development of the claim or topic that is **consistently appropriate** to the task by using **clear and convincing** reasoning supported by **relevant textual** evidence; demonstrates **purposeful** coherence, clarity, and cohesion, making it **easy to follow** the writer's progression of ideas; establishes and maintains an **effective** style, attending to the norms and conventions of the discipline.
Score Point 3	The student response addresses the prompt and provides **mostly effective** development of the claim or topic that is **mostly appropriate** to the task, by using **clear** reasoning supported by **relevant textual** evidence; demonstrates coherence, clarity, and cohesion, making it **fairly easy to follow** the writer's progression of ideas; establishes and maintains a **mostly effective** style, while attending to the norms and conventions of the discipline.
Score Point 2	The student response addresses the prompt and provides **some** development of the claim or topic that is **somewhat appropriate** to the task, by using **some** reasoning and **text-based** evidence; demonstrates **some** coherence, clarity, and/or cohesion, making the writer's progression of ideas **usually discernible but not obvious**; has a style that is **somewhat** effective, **generally** attending to the norms and conventions of the discipline.
Score Point 1	The student response addresses the prompt and provides **minimal** development of the claim or topic that is **limited in its appropriateness** to the task by using **limited** reasoning and **text-based** evidence. Or the response is a developed, text-based response with **little or no awareness** of the prompt; demonstrates **limited** coherence, clarity, and/or cohesion, making the writer's progression of ideas **somewhat unclear**, has a style that has **limited** effectiveness, with **limited** awareness of the norms of the discipline.
Score Point 0	The student response is **undeveloped** and/or **inappropriate** to the task; **lacks** coherence, clarity, and cohesion; has an **inappropriate** style, with **little to no** awareness of the norms of the discipline.